MISUNDERSTOOD

From Neo Nazi Hooligan in the *Town of Flowers*, to Black Excellence

Ben J. Butler

Misunderstood
Ben Butler Ben Butler

©Ben J. Butler 2025
Front cover design: Krisography
Back Cover Design: Marcia M Publishing House
First draft preparation: Aurea Reis
Foreword by Joanna Oliver
Manuscript development and Editorial Coordination Marcia M. Spence
Edited by the Marcia M Publishing House editorial team.
All rights reserved 2025 Ben J. Butler
Ben J. Butler asserts the moral right to be identified as the author of this work. The opinions expressed in this published work are those of the author and do not reflect the opinions of Marcia M Publishing House or its editorial team.

Published by Marcia M Spence via Marcia M Publishing House, author services, West Bromwich, UNITED KINGDOM, on behalf of Ben J. Butler

Email: info@marciampublishing.com

This book is sold subject to the conditions that it is not, by way of trade or otherwise, lent, hired out or otherwise circulated in any form of binding or cover other than that in which it is published. No part of this publication may be reproduced, stored in a retrieval system, or transmitted in any form or by any means (electronic, mechanical, photocopying, recording or otherwise) without prior written permission from the Author. This memoir is written from the author's recollection of events as told to the writers and editorial team.

ISBN: 978-1-9193441-2-6

A copy of this publication is legally deposited in The British Library.

www.marciampublishing.com

DEDICATION

To my grandparents.

Reflecting on my journey, I am often filled with sadness and longing that my grandparents are no longer here to witness the person I have become or to read the words I have written Ain this book.

There is a part of me that truly hopes, wherever they may be, they can somehow see their grandson's progress and take pride in the man I am striving to be.

My greatest wish is that I am making them proud, especially considering all the hardships and heartache I may have caused them in the past. There were many occasions when my actions left them disappointed or upset, and for those times, I am deeply sorry. Now, as I look back and see the positive impact I am making within the Shropshire community, I hope they can recognise the good I am working to achieve.

The depth of my love and the sense of loss I feel for them is beyond words, there are no words strong enough to capture how much I miss them.

This book stands as a reflection of their influence on my life, and it is with all my heart that I dedicate it to both of them.

To My Children

I also extend this dedication to my children, who mean the world to me and who I love dearly.

To Friends and Family Lost

To suicide, murder and ill health, you will always be in my heart and thoughts.

ACKNOWLEDGEMENTS

My friends, family and my network. Vicki S., Joe Plomer, The Springfield lads, Kevin Bartlett, Rob Wilson, Ben P, Recharge, The Prince's Trust, Nina & Co, Caymen and sons, Jenny C, Dolores, Darryl Laycock Darryl Jay, Shaun P, Adam P & Co, Tony P, Sarah S, Laura Hollie, Darren Edwards, Mental Health Team, Auntie Ally, Craig Walton, TAARC, Gem Heywood, My Therapist, Joanna C, The Herd, Mark J, Baldy Lewis, Enable, Sean O'hanlon,H4H, Royal British Legion, Band of Brothers, Joanna Oliver, Tim Allin, El Gringo, The Talking Tradesmen, Dribbz , and Danielle John, Smidy, BLAC AWARDS, Andy Murphy, Jack Griffiths, Nutrain Body, Darren Howells, Tony Rianna, Kim Harris, James M, James Hetihewa,

To anyone else that has helped me on my path to become a better person, better Father and better judge of character thank you

Kristography — Thank you for designing the front cover which perfectly represents my story.

Aurea Reis — Thank you for working with me to get my story on paper by preparing the first draft of this book before it went to the publisher.

Jannette Barrett — For the production of the play.

Joanna Oliver — for your connection, support and for writing the foreword for my book

Marcia M. Spence and **The Marcia M Publishing House** team of editors and writers, thank you for your guidance and support through this process.

FOREWORD
By Joanna Oliver

I first connected with Ben in 2020 on LinkedIn, when he reached out to me to see if I could help him to raise funds for the work he was doing Mentoring young people. My first words were, "I have looked at your profile...what a journey! Congrats on turning your life around." Since then, I have seen in a multitude of ways how Ben has grown and throughout it all, he has remained consistent in his authentic identity. There is always a sense of, "what you see is what you get" with Ben.

I would say that our paths were destined to cross because to my amazement, Ben is from Telford, which is my hometown, where I was born and grew up. Some of Ben's experiences, especially related to racial abuse, completely resonate. It wasn't easy growing up Black in 'Telford New Town' in the 70s and 80s, let alone without the multiple horrors Ben faced.

Ben has always been really open with me about his challenges, derived from his adverse childhood experiences and if I were to share one dominant message about Ben, it would be that he acknowledges his vulnerability, whilst walking in his strength.

In many ways, Ben embodies the whole spectrum of adversity, from a range of abuse forms, domestic violence, the care system, drug abuse, mental ill-health and neurodivergence, alongside criminal exploitation and enduring incarceration in the criminal justice system. I was thankful to Ben, for agreeing to be interviewed as one of my research collaborators for my doctoral narrative research, documenting the experiences of the criminal justice system, for Black young men who are autistic. Ben's words will always ring in my ears, "I learned to be Black in prison", a shocking truth that reflects failings in our society.

Not only has Ben transmuted learning from his experiences to improve his own life but to generate cultural capital, in engaging young people in schools and those who are care experienced. As someone who knows first-hand, the pervasive nature of trauma, Ben is a credible messenger for these young people, who very often may feel like no one really understands them.

My high regard for Ben is unending and to bear witness to this book, spoken of early on in our relationship and then having the honour of writing the foreword to that book, is a complete honour and privilege. Thank you, Ben, for trusting me.

MISUNDERSTOOD

From Neo Nazi Hooligan in the *Town of Flowers*, to Black Excellence

Ben J. Butler

Contents

Foreword *By Joanna Oliver* 10

1. Fish, Chips and MJ 17

2. The Turning Point! 24

3. A Kid Pretending to Be a Man 31

4. Violence My Lover 39

5. Sentenced 53

6. Stuck in the cycle 63

7. Sex & Drugs 73

8. Life in the Army 79

9. Trying to Rebuild 85

10. What's Effing Wrong With Me? 92

11. Where I Am Now & My Future Aspirations 95

Afterword 99

Testimonials and Endorsements. 103

Gallery. 122

About the Author 134

1. FISH, CHIPS AND MJ

I was born in 1986, in Shrewsbury, Shropshire. My mum raised me on her own, though really, it was my grandparents who raised me too. For a while, me and Mum lived at their house, on the living room floor, curled up in a sleeping bag. I can still picture the thick carpet smell mixed with tea and toast, the sound of my grandad's slippers dragging to the kettle every morning.

My grandparents were my world. They took me to church on Fridays and Sundays. Fridays were for mass in the evening, then we'd do the pools round. I was about five when I started going with them, and I did it for years. I loved it. After the round, we'd stop for fish and chips, and I'd get to sip a little glass of Pale Cream Sherry. It made me feel grown up. At Christmas time, all the customers would give us tips or little presents, tins of biscuits, maybe a scarf or a box of chocolates. It always used to be Fish Friday. We were Catholics, so fish was tradition, but it was  more than that. It was family. It was warmth. Those early years were happy. My grandparents' house was full of people, noise, laughter, cousins, and always food on the go. They even had a tortoise called Flash that used to wander around the garden like he owned the place.

When Mum left for university on Sundays, I used to cry for days. My auntie says they couldn't calm me down until Friday came around again and Mum was back. It went on like that for four years while she did Business Studies. When she was home for the holidays, I stayed with her in her student accommodation. Her friends, Angela and Jane the Brain,  became like my aunties. They were fun, loud, always laughing, always kind. Auntie Angela still sends me Christmas and birthday cards even now. Those memories feel like warm light when I look back. I can still see myself in the bath at her place, splashing about with a plastic crocodile toy. Simple moments, but they stuck.

When Mum finally got her own place, it was in Monkmoor Flats, across from the old Job Centre. That's where things started to change. That's where the bad memories begin.

The first time I remember being hurt was a Sunday after church. We were all in the car, me, Mum, my uncle, and my grandparents. Michael Jackson was on the radio, and I was obsessed with him. Still am, really. But we got home before the song finished. I didn't want to get out yet; I wanted to hear the end. I leaned forward from the back seat to get closer to the sound. My hand was by the car door, near Mum's side. I saw it in her eyes before it happened, that flash of anger. Then she slammed the door. The pain was instant. My fingers crushed, bleeding. My middle finger was the worst. Even now, I can remember that pain, and her face more than the hurt itself.

The second time is harder to talk about. It was about food. I've always had a difficult relationship with eating. If I don't feel safe or comfortable, I can't eat. I was only six when she told me that if I didn't eat my tea, she'd make me eat a bowl of wool used for knitting. And she did. I remember trying to chew, the roughness in my mouth, it wasn't something made to eat, it made me choke. Then everything goes blank.

After she got together with her partner, it only got worse. The good moments disappeared. The only times I was happy were when I stayed with my grandparents. There was just one holiday to Greece. The only memory of us four being happy together. I don't even think I was happy because of them, it was because I met a girl and we spent most days together, it was two sisters and we would be away from our parents most of the time. Sunshine, blue water, and laughter that didn't hurt. But it didn't last.

I went to Springfield Infant School, near my grandparents' house. School was rough. I went through a lot of racial abuse. The other kids would pour milk over my head, bite me and call me names. I was the only child of colour there, and I stood out in all the wrong ways. Still, I had one mate. He was poor like me, and we bonded over that, I knew that he didn't go on holidays in the summer, it would be me and him available to play all through the holidays when other went away with their families. When everyone came back from their fancy holidays, we made up stories about going to South Africa to see Jurassic Park together. We were obsessed with dinosaurs. That was our escape, our way of feeling like we belonged somewhere, even if it was pretend.

There were good parts too. Mrs. Patterson, my teacher, was amazing. She wasn't white she was a black woman,

Jamaican or South African maybe, and she was the first Black person I'd ever known. She made me feel safe. I used to massage her feet while she read us stories, and she'd let me sit right at the front. It made me feel special, like she saw me. It sounds absurd now, but for me it was comfort. It was closeness. She made me feel seen and cared for. Something my mother never did.

I kissed girls in the playhouse too; we were only six, but it felt like the start of something secret and exciting. I was always curious about girls.

As a kid, I loved football and rugby. Sports made sense to me; they gave me something to be good at, something to belong to. I loved Michael Jackson too. He wasn't just an artist; he was magic. I taught my little brother how to do MJ's moves. I'd wear my glasses, one glove, and a jacket, and just lose myself in the music. I was filmed dancing at one of Mum's friend's weddings once. Everyone cheering, clapping. I felt alive. I was a dancer. MJ was my hero.

I played rugby for the under-16s, a left winger. I was quick. People thought I could've gone pro. Maybe I could've. Then I switched to football. Maybe I could've gone semi-pro if I'd focused more. But life had a way of distracting me. I also loved writing stories, inventing worlds. My imagination was huge back then. As I've grown older, I've found it harder, like that part of me got quieter somehow.

I loved cricket, kerby, tag and all the street games. My friends and I rode bikes everywhere. My grandparents bought me a silver Peugeot bike with front springs, and I thought it was the best thing in the world. We'd ride all over Shrewsbury, exploring every alley and park we could find. Wednesdays were shopping list days for Nan and Grandad. Fridays were shopping days. Nan always bought my favourites, Pot Noodles and cookies. I was spoiled, really. They looked after me like I *was* their son. In truth, they were my parents in all the ways that mattered.

Saturday mornings were my favourite. I'd come downstairs, wrap myself in a blanket, and watch *Soccer AM* with my hot chocolate and cookies. I could always eat at my grandparents' house. Food felt safe there. Grandad used to make up stories he called *Tales of the Riverbank*. He'd tickle my head as he told them until I fell asleep. I do that with my daughter now. Some things stay with you, no matter what. I went to many football matches with my Grandad I always supported Shrewsbury Town.

I've been told that when I was three or four, I once drove Grandad's green BMW into the garage and broke his arm chasing me up the cold bank. I don't remember it clearly, but it sounds like something I'd do. I remember sitting on the kitchen counter watching Nan bake bread. I'd sneak bits of dough and eat them while they rose in front of the coal fire. That fire was my favourite spot, a blanket, pillow, warmth. That was home.

Music filled my world too. After Michael Jackson came Eminem; his songs made sense to me. *Sing for the Moment* still hits me hard: about his dad not being there, the anger, the confusion, the pain from home. It was like someone else finally said what I couldn't. I also listened to 2Pac, 50 Cent, Biggie, Oasis, The Stone Roses, Madness, D12, all of them are the soundtracks of my childhood. Sometimes I'd switch to Red Hot Chili Peppers or The Libertines. Old-school nineties stuff, *Rhythm Is a Dancer*, *Black Box*. That was my dancing music. I didn't like the hardcore rave stuff that blasted from the younger lads' stereos. I needed melody, rhythm, feeling. And the rap music scene, Nas, Mobb Deep and the Wu Tang Clan.

Eventually, we moved again. New house, new school. And that's where the madness really began.

2. THE TURNING POINT!

In 1992 we moved to Greenfields. 44 Percy Street, a place that always felt like darkness. From outside, it was nothing special, just another red-brick terrace with tired curtains and a gate that creaked every time you opened it. But inside, something was always tense. You could almost feel the house itself waiting for the arguments to start again.

I had mates around there though, good lads mostly, and the street was our playground. We'd play Kerby till the streetlights came on, using an old football that had lost half its colour. We'd run up and down the road, yelling, laughing, daring each other to nick conkers from next door's tree or climb onto the garage roof. Sometimes we played *"Knock Door Bunk,"* tying fishing wire to door knockers and hiding round corners while the neighbours shouted. It was stupid, harmless mischief, and it was freedom, the only freedom I had back then.

Next to Greenfields was Ditherington estate, rougher, louder, the kind of estate where everyone knew everyone's business. That's where I got the nickname *Black Magic*. I was the only mixed-race kid around, and the name stuck. It wasn't meant kindly, but I learned to wear it like armour. Better to laugh and nod along than to show it stung.

In the summer the hours stretched out between one meal and the next; they were long, but nights were short. The night, that's when it all started again. The shouting. The thuds. My mum and her fella tearing into each other like enemies.

Mum worked at BT back then. Her fella drank the potent stuff; cheap vodka, whisky, anything that burned, and she'd pour herself glass after glass of wine, telling herself she was coping. I'd sit on the bottom few steps, half hidden behind the banister, heart pounding while their voices rose and fell. Sometimes I thought about running out into the street, knocking on a neighbour's door. But what would I say? So, I just sat there, listening, small and scared. There was no escape.

I could tell when it was about to turn physical; the sound in Mum's voice changed. I'd hear a crash, a scuffle, the dull sound of something, or someone, hitting the wall. I'd press my hands over my ears but it didn't block it out. Even now, certain noises take me straight back to that hallway.

My stepdad never came round to my grandparents' house. Nan said she never liked him, said there was something off about him. Years later I realised she was right. There was a time when my uncle Lee and his partner even talked about adopting me. They saw what was happening, but back then people didn't talk about things like that. You were just expected to "get on with it."

When things got really bad, my little brother would wet the bed. He'd cry, shaking, whispering my name. I'd lift him up, his pyjamas cold and damp, and carry him into my bed. I'd lie next to him until his breathing steadied, and then, when I was sure he was asleep, I'd sneak into Mum's room. I'd lie on her side of the bed, where it still smelled of her perfume. A mix of smoke and something floral.

There was a red digital clock on her bedside table. The numbers glowed like little embers in the dark. I'd watch them change - 3:14, 3:15, 3:16 - counting down the hours until she got up for work. When the alarm went off at half six, I'd roll under the bed, heart hammering, waiting for the sound of her footsteps to fade down the stairs. Only then would I crawl back to my room, like nothing had happened.

My brother Lee was born in 1992. Blonde hair, blue eyes, his dad was white. I was five years older, darker-skinned, with curly hair that wouldn't stay down no matter how much I brushed it. Mum used to say she loved my skin, but she didn't treat me the same. I could feel the difference every day. How she spoke to me, how she looked at me when I did something wrong.

One day she lost it with Lee, threw a hard-back book straight at him. It hit his eye. The noise he made, a sharp little cry, stuck with me. Then she turned to me and said, "You, did it. Tell them you did it." I was only a kid, but I did what she said. I went to school and told Miss Williams that it was me. I remember the disbelief on her face. I remember how sick I felt lying to protect Mum.

At school I started making little weapons; pencils sharpened at both ends, rulers wrapped in tape, things I didn't even plan to use. It just made me feel safe having them. Like if something went wrong, I could do something back. At home, my stepdad made sure to hit me where it didn't show. Punches to the stomach, ribs, thighs. The pain that you feel the next morning is more than when it happens.

Mum wasn't innocent either. Once she shoved my head into the sink and held it down. The shock of cold water, the smell of bleach, the sound of my own muffled screams. *I can still feel that moment in my bones.* When she finally let go, I gasped like I'd been underwater for hours.

I think that's when I detached from things. It's like I was there, but not there. Watching from outside myself.

By the age of ten or eleven, I'd started smoking weed. It wasn't about being cool; it was about being numb. About quieting the noise.

One afternoon my stepdad asked if I was "on something?" Mum was home, which was rare that early in the day. I told them both to fuck off. He chased me up the stairs, tripped me near the bathroom. I landed on the door hard, and Mum appeared out of nowhere and started kicking me in the head. I didn't even recognise her face. It was like she'd turned into someone else.

When it was over, I lay there on the landing, dizzy, staring at the wallpaper. The flowers on it seemed to move. Something inside me broke that day. After that, I stopped crying. I stopped expecting things to get better.

They grounded me for weeks. I'd sit in my room, staring out the window, watching my brother play outside. I'd tap on the glass, hoping he'd look up, but he never did.

That's when I first remember thinking, *maybe I don't belong anywhere.*

When I was about twelve, I spent most of my time at a friend's house. They were often racist toward me, calling me "darky" and other things. I didn't feel like I fitted in anywhere.

Me and my friend used to go to this older guy's house. He was a Neo-Nazi in his mid-forties named Rab. He had "SKINS" tattooed across his forehead and a swastika on his hand. He was a heavy drug user, had no teeth, and would even liquidise drugs to use them. I'm Black, so you can imagine how strange and unsettling it was to be around someone like that, but at the time it felt normal because we had nowhere else to go.

We would hang around his place, taking pills and smoking weed. One day we walked in, and his fifteen- or sixteen-year-old daughter was lying on the bed, high on heroin. She was already addicted. We sat there next to her, smoking like it was just another day. At that age, we had already normalised things no kid should ever see.

I can still remember being grounded, staring out my bedroom window while watching my friends play outside. My brother was never grounded; it was always only me. I saw how he was loved, and I felt like I wasn't cared for at all. I didn't know who to turn to.

That's why I loved going to my nan and grandad's. Their house felt safe. But whenever I stayed there, my mum would call and ask them to send me home. She'd promise over the phone that things would get better, that things would change. But they never did. Nothing changed.

Percy Street

3. A KID PRETENDING TO BE A MAN

It happened near the river that cut through the estate like a scar. My mate rang me, said some lads had jumped him. I didn't even ask who or why. You didn't in those days. Loyalty was automatic.

It was early evening, the damp Shrewsbury night where the air smells of mud and iron. My mate's lip was split, his eye already swelling. "They're down there," he said, nodding towards the bend in the river.

We walked quietly, hoods up, trainers crunching on gravel. You could hear the water moving, slow.

There were three or four of them by the bank, smoking, and laughing. One saw us and called out, "What you saying then?"

And that was it! No build-up, no warning. Just fists. Mud, shouts, splashes, breath turning to steam. Someone grabbed my hood and yanked me backwards; I spun, swung wildly, connected with something soft. I heard a grunt, felt knuckles split against skin.

I ended up grappling with one lad right at the edge. The river smell was strong, like rotting weeds and cold metal. He hit me across the ear and the world went white. I shoved him back; he slipped and scrambled up again. Then there was a shout, "Police!" Everyone scattered.

As we were walking off, still buzzing, my mate stopped and pointed. "What's that on your leg?"

I looked down. Something was sticking out of the back of my calf. At first I thought it was a twig. I reached back and touched it. It was glass. The neck of a broken bottle. At first I felt nothing, just numb shock. Then the heat came, a deep burning pain that made my stomach twist. Blood ran into my sock, warm and sticky. I said, "What the fuck," and the others crowded round.

Someone shouted, "Leave it in!" but I'd already pulled it. The sound it made, a wet pop, will never leave me. Blood sprayed onto the dirt, dark and thick. I wrapped my T-shirt around the wound, pulling tight. My mate said I needed hospital. I said, "Nah, I'm fine." Didn't want to look weak. Didn't want to explain.

I limped away from the river, laughing loudly, pretending it was nothing. Every step was fire. The blood kept coming, soaking through the fabric, dripping onto my one trainer. I could feel it squelch when I walked.

When I got home, I washed it in the sink. The water went pink, then red. The cut was long and jagged, like someone had carved a smile into my leg.

I didn't go to hospital. Just wrapped it tighter and went to bed.

By morning my jeans had stuck to the wound. Peeling them off hurt worse than the stabbing. I remember laughing while tears ran down my face. That was the kind of boy I'd become, hurting and laughing at the same time.

After that, I walked differently. Thought different. I wasn't invincible, but I started acting like I was. Every time I looked at the scar, I felt both proud and scared. Proud that I'd survived. Scared of what I was turning into.

After that night by the river, something in me hardened. I stopped flinching when people shouted. I stopped caring what happened next. The scar on my leg became part of me, proof that pain didn't kill you, that it could even make you feel alive for a while.

I started carrying knives. At first, I told myself it was just for cutting up resin, but that wasn't the truth. It was for safety, or at least the idea of safety. Having it in my pocket made me feel less powerless.

By then, the police already knew my name. My school records had red flags everywhere! "aggressive behaviour," "poor attendance," "possible domestic issues." I was categorised as 'A Child In Need', meaning I needed monitoring and my family needed support. I had a social worker who came to see me now and then and he took me to places like McDonald's and to Cafés for coffees. He was nice enough, always wore a suit, always smelled clean. He'd sit across from me with his notepad, asking how things were at home.

I never told him anything real. I didn't trust him. He wasn't one of us. Years later, we met again by chance, and he laughed when I told him why I never spoke to him. I said, "You weren't black. You'd never lived it. And you wore a suit."

MISUNDERSTOOD

He said he understood, but I don't think he really did.

I was drifting; I was running away some nights, staying at mates' houses or down by the train tracks where the lines split. There was an abandoned building there with smashed windows and graffiti all over the walls. We turned it into our place. Dragged in old sofas, found a radio, even a grill. We had our own little world. We'd sit there all night, smoking, drinking cheap cider, playing music through a bust speaker, pretending the world outside didn't exist. For those few hours, I could breathe. Then I'd go home, and it would all start again, the shouting, the fear, the fists.

That's when I started selling resin for Rab. I knew it wasn't smart, but it gave me money, gave me purpose. I didn't feel small when I was doing something grown.

One night, my stepdad grabbed me by the throat during another fight. I could feel my pulse beating against his hand. I reached for the knife in my pocket, not even thinking. I swung it up, but the blade snapped against his arm, cheap metal. It didn't even break his skin. He called the police anyway. They charged me with ABH and gave me a reprimand. I was eleven. After that, I stopped pretending to be the victim. I told myself I was the one in control now. Every bruise felt like a reason to fight harder. Every insult felt like a dare.

By fourteen, fifteen, I'd been stabbed, arrested, grounded, beaten, and somehow, I thought I was winning. That's when everything blurred together, gangs, drugs, fights, nights that ended in flashing blue lights. I didn't see it as danger; I saw it as belonging.

It was a warm summer afternoon, the kind where everything smells of smoke and grass. Someone's mum was out, so we had the garden to ourselves. Music blasting, cheap cider in plastic cups, everyone laughing too loud. For once, I felt light. Just another lad having a good time.

Then he showed up. The same lad who used to drag me down the stairs years before, calling me names, spitting on me, making me feel less than human. He came swaggering in like he owned the place, shouting, joking, showing off. The laughter died down as soon as he spoke. Everyone could feel the shift.

I tried to ignore him. I really did. I'd grown used to swallowing things, keeping them inside. But then he started mouthing off about my mate's sister, some nasty stuff. He laughed like it was nothing.

That's when I felt something snap inside me. I was holding a BBQ skewer, still warm from the grill. I remember looking at it, feeling the heat through the metal, hearing the sizzle of meat still clinging to the tip. Then I looked at him. He smirked, like he knew I wouldn't do anything. I didn't even think. My arm just moved. The sound it made when it hit him was a half pop, half hiss that will never leave me. He screamed, clutching his arm. People shouted, someone dropped a can, and the music kept playing for a second before someone turned it off. The smell of burnt meat mixed with blood and smoke.

He ran off through the back gate, bleeding. I just stood there, skewer still in my hand, heart thudding so loud it drowned everything else out.

Part of me felt strong. Part of me felt sick.

Later, when the police came, I didn't resist. They said, "racially aggravated assault." The irony of that hit me like another punch. The only black kid, charged with a racial assault.

In the cell, everything was quiet. Just me, the hum of the light, and that slow, echoing drip from the tap. I remember staring at the wall and seeing everything at once; my mum's face twisted with anger, my stepdad's fists, Rab's yellow curtains, the flash of the river, that lad's face when the skewer hit. It all ran together into one feeling: anger. But underneath that anger, there was something else. Something small and frightened. I didn't want to admit it, even to myself.

When I got out, the story had already spread. Lads who'd barely spoken to me before were nodding, clapping my shoulder, calling me a "mad bastard." Older ones invited me to drink with them, come to football matches, stand with the crowd. They talked about loyalty, about never backing down, about brotherhood. For the first time, I felt seen. Not loved. Just seen. They gave me new trainers, free drinks, and a sense that I mattered.

When everyone went home, I'd sit awake, staring at the scar on my leg or the scab on my knuckles, wondering if this was it. If this was who I was now.

A fighter. A liar. A kid pretending to be a man. Some nights, I'd scrub my skin raw, wishing I could scrape off everything. The memories, the fear, even my colour. I didn't know who I was. Not white enough. Not black enough. Just angry, tired, and lost.

4. VIOLENCE MY LOVER

My life of crime involved knife crime and weapons; I still remember the cold, metallic weight of my first gun, clutched in my sweaty seventeen-year-old hands. The smell of oil and metal lingered on my fingers, a scent I couldn't wash off no matter how hard I scrubbed. I chose crime because I never truly felt accepted, either at home, where the air was thick with tension and the sharp tang of arguments, or outside, where I was always too different.

As I mentioned before, one day I bumped into my friend. That was the day I shaved my head, the vibrating razor biting against my scalp, each pass revealing more of my bare skin and sending a shiver down my spine. It was as if I was shedding a layer, trying to find someone else underneath.

I then went to my first football match against Telford. In the stadium, the roar of the crowd vibrated, the smell of cheap lager and fried onions thick in the cold evening air. My heart hammered as I pressed forward with the others, every sense sharpened. The electric tension before the fight, the rush of bodies, fists colliding, the taste of blood in my mouth mixing with the metallic tang of adrenaline. In the chaos, I felt alive surrounded by a pack of lads who wanted exactly what I did, who craved that explosive release. For the first time, I belonged, the shouts and chants wrapping around me like armour, drowning out everything else.

Getting involved in football violence became a routine part of my life. Every week, we'd meet up, usually at the local pub, to talk about where and when we'd fight other football gangs. It didn't matter if we played at home or away.

Even though I was spending more time with the football crew, I still had my own problems on the estate. I split my time between the lads and my old friends, but I never felt like I truly belonged to either group. Trouble seemed to follow me everywhere. I remember tense nights, like the

BBQ in Sandbourne that turned into a fight, and other nights that ended badly, leaving both physical and emotional scars.

My violence got more serious, and I was charged twice for violent crimes, wounding and disorder. The last time, I ended up in Stoke Heath prison on remand, which changed everything for me.

One big event happened during the Shrewsbury versus Telford youth cup match. We wanted to meet a group of older lads, but before we could, things changed and we went to the Old Butcherly pub in Shrewsbury. I was with one of my best friends, who has since died. He wanted a smoke, so we asked a group of three men outside for a lighter, but they were rude. We were drinking cider, and one of my mates got angry and threw a bottle at them. They went inside the pub, into the kitchen, and I followed. That's when a big fight broke out. We hit them with metal bars and kicked them. Afterward, we ran towards the train station, but we got caught. That's when I realised how deep I was in this life.

We were all arrested and remanded in custody for three days. It was a cold, relentless blur. those hours ticking by more slowly than I thought possible, the chill of the cell chilling deep into my bones. I've been convicted of fourteen crimes, mostly involving violence and weapons, but this time, the weight of what I'd done hit more heavily than ever. The three-day remand left me quite nervous; my mind raced with what-ifs and worst-case scenarios, each minute adding another layer of dread. That usually means that you will be remanded to prison.

So, we went to court. We all were remanded in custody at Stoke Heath, but I hadn't been to my house for ten days. When I finally rang my mum from Stoke Heath prison, hearing her voice break into sobs on the other end of the line shattered me. She was crying because she had not seen me for ten days, her worry, and heartbreak pouring through the phone, making me feel smaller, more lost than ever. All the bravado, all the anger faded in that moment, replaced by guilt I couldn't ignore. I spent a lot of my time away from home because of all the violence that was happening at home, but in that instant, I realised how much pain I'd caused her. The violence wasn't just scarring me; it was also tearing my family apart.

Mum was going through a divorce, and I had lost myself in the haze of late-night parties, the cheap spirits, and the thumping bass. I started selling Coke and Crack, plastic bags filled with white powder that smelled faintly of chemicals and money.

My life of crime involved knives and weapons. I still remember holding my first gun when I was seventeen, feeling nervous as I gripped the cold metal. The smell of oil and metal stuck to my hands, no matter how much I washed them. I chose crime because I never felt accepted at home. There were always arguments, and outside I always felt different.

The first time the prison doors shut behind me, the loud noise scared me. I could hear other prisoners banging on the pipes, trying to frighten me. My heart raced, my mouth went dry, and my hands shook. Anyone who says they weren't scared the first time they went to prison is lying. Everyone I spoke to in prison shared similar feelings. When the cell door closed, you noticed inmates convicted of various crimes, murderers, and sex offenders alike, all were housed together. The atmosphere was a heavy mix of anxiety and acceptance of our fates, with little privacy and constant tension. Conversations often revolved around survival tactics and adjusting to life behind bars., regardless of background or crime, everyone was forced to adapt to the same challenging conditions within those walls.

I was classed as a high-risk offender, so I wasn't able to be partnered out with anyone. This meant that, unlike some inmates who could share a cell or take part in certain activities with a 'padmate', I was kept isolated for much of my time in prison. The authorities believed that my past convictions for violent offences and my reputation both inside and outside prison made me a potential risk to others. As a result, I was often placed in single cells and had restricted access to communal spaces, which intensified my sense of isolation.

Being labelled as high-risk also affected how the prison staff interacted with me. There was a constant air of caution, and I felt as though I was always under scrutiny. Even during routine activities like collecting meals or attending education sessions, officers kept a closer watch on me than on other inmates. This status not only limited my opportunities for social interaction, but it also made it harder to build trust with others on the wing. In a place already rife with suspicion and tension, being singled out in this way made prison life that much more challenging and lonelier.

I spent three months on remand before I was sentenced. During this period at Stoke Heath, I found myself involved in a few altercations, which seemed almost inevitable in the tense environment. The necessity of standing your ground and show strength was ever-present. Prison was a place where you had to fight to earn recognition and respect from others.

Despite the violence, I developed close bonds with some inmates. One was serving time for attempted murder and another, for armed robbery. The shared experiences and constant threat of conflict brought us together.

After my time on remand, I was released from Stoke Heath, awaiting my final sentencing. My release came with strict conditions: I was *on tag* each day only until 19:00. The uncertainty of the pending sentencing hung over me.

That didn't deter me away from crime. I was arrested on three occasions for two section 18 offences, GBH, and affray. Even after facing the harsh reality of a prison sentence and feeling the consequences of my actions, I found myself pulled back into the same destructive patterns, unable to break free from the cycle that had defined so much of my life. The streets still called me, and the need for acceptance and respect amongst my peers remained a powerful force, fuelling more reckless choices and keeping me firmly rooted in a world where violence and crime felt almost inevitable.

That day at The Plough Pub lingers in my mind, not just for the violence but for the way it exposed the thin line between friendship and rivalry in our world. The chaos outside the pub made it clear how unpredictable things had become. Those we called mates one moment could turn into enemies the next, all because of a look, a word, or the wrong allegiance. The shock on the faces of the new pub owners was a stark reminder that our actions had consequences beyond our circles; we were changing the atmosphere of the entire community, instilling fear where there used to be normality. Yet even after seeing blood spilled in front of me, with police always lurking and the threat of retribution never far away, I still couldn't pull myself out of that life. The cycle of violence, the lure of the next rush, and the feeling of being part of something bigger kept me coming back, no matter the cost.

That night, when my friend was taken to the hospital, a wave of guilt and relief crashed over me. I was relieved he was okay, but I couldn't shake the image of blood and panic, the fear that something irreversible might have happened. The tension of those moments clung to me like a second skin, amplifying my dread and intensifying the emptiness I felt when the dust finally settled.

We then had a pub in Belview called the Masonic. That's where I was stabbed on the top of my head with the end of a bottle. There was a fight, and someone properly stabbed the end of a bottle in my head right in the pub. I was taken to the hospital; I was glued and stitched up.

My mate took me. I had stitches on the top of my head. I was discharged from the hospital soon after that happened. I went out to a party, selling and taking drugs while partying.

The cycle of violence, the lure of the next rush, and the feeling of being part of something bigger kept me coming back, no matter the cost. There was a twisted comfort in the chaos. A sense that, even when everything else fell apart, the adrenaline of violence and danger was always there to steady me. Each fight, each reckless act, felt like a desperate grab for meaning, for belonging.

During the football days, it was like two different lives. On one side you had the pitch, the lads, the shout, and the banter. On the other side, you had this undercurrent of hate from some of the older football lads. Not all of them, but enough. It got worse when I started going out with a girl from the same circle. That set off something ugly. She wasn't from the nicest family, and some of those older men couldn't stand the idea of a black lad being with their stepdaughter. You couldn't tell me this would end quietly. It exploded!

The trouble started with sneers, shots across the head, things whispered when I walked past. Then it moved into pushes and shoves, then proper confrontations. Within six months it had escalated so much that a bunch of us were in trouble with the law. Fifteen of us ended up facing sentencing. A mad number. Everyone I used to hang around with was in it for different things, different charges, but they came at us hard. The Crown wanted the worst offenders, so they aimed to pull out the ones who'd cause the most trouble. We all stuck close to each other while we could, because out there the only people who had your back were the people who'd been in the same mess.

I remember the phone call. My solicitor ringing in the early morning; the ringtone cutting through my sleep. "You've got to appear at Crown Court tomorrow," he said. "Sentencing." I couldn't breathe properly after that. Fifteen of us. Sitting in that dock, watching people get called, watching faces turn from boys to something else. The court was cold, hard benches, the echo of shoes, the judge's voice like a guillotine. They read out names, charges, and our stories. My name sounded strange, like someone else's name. I felt small.

They handed sentences down. For me, it was under two years at first, and then an extra eight months for an affray tied to the football stuff. All together it added up to just over thirty-four months. Obviously you do half of it; that's how it worked, so I came out after serving the part I was meant to. I'd been in and out of courts before, but standing there with the cell door clanging shut behind you, that's different. You feel the weight of it then.

Prison fixed nothing. If anything, it sharpened the edges. I met people in there who were proper into gangs, and they had time, and stories, and ways of looking at the world that hooked into the anger I already had. You get time to sit and talk and learn and be shown things. I met lads who taught me how to carry myself, how to survive, how to not be soft. It felt like training.

And then there was the damage that came with it. I've been stabbed twice, proper, ugly times when the air seemed to be knocked clean out of me. My nose got broken one time; another time my teeth were smashed, and now I've got three false teeth. I've had my head stomped on so hard the hospital had to stitch me up and check me for brain injury. Once there were teeth stuck in my hand after I put it where it shouldn't have been. Knuckles broken, scars all over my hands, marks down my arms. I could name a dozen places on my body where things happened. I can still point to and say, "That was when…"

They are trophies and warnings at the same time. Sometimes I tell myself I earned them, that I was taking my anger out in the only way I knew. Other times I look and think I just made holes in my body and my life. For a while, I enjoyed the badness; it felt like purpose. When you're angry and scared, being the person who others fear gives you a kind of power you don't get at home.

There was another time, another fight that still plays back in flashes. I was drunk, properly gone. the kind of drunk where the world tilts and nothing feels real. I saw these lads messing around with a bike, and for some reason I thought it was mine. Maybe I wanted it to be. Maybe I just wanted trouble. I tried to take it, and they beat me for it. Boots, fists, the sound of laughter that wasn't funny.

I went home bleeding, drunk and dizzy, but my head wouldn't stop spinning with payback. That's how I was wired the. Every hit had to be answered. I sat there planning it out, thinking, *I'll get them one by one.* And I did. Three of them, one by one, caught off guard, little bursts of revenge that didn't fix a thing. Each one left me feeling emptier.

Then came the night that could have changed everything. There was a house party, music booming, lights flashing off bottles and walls.

One lad who'd jumped me was there; he didn't even know I was in the house. My chest tightened as soon as I saw him. All the noise faded out, replaced by thoughts of revenge.

I walked into the kitchen. There was a knife on the counter. It was one of those long ones with a black handle. I picked it up without even thinking. My hand just closed around it like it belonged there. I walked back out; the blade catching the light. Someone shouted, "Drop the knife!" but the voice came from far away, like I was underwater.

I didn't drop it. I swung. The knife cut through his jacket. Only half an inch away from changing both our lives forever. I still don't know how it missed. Maybe luck. Maybe something stopped me at the last second. When I saw his face twist in shock, I dropped the knife. Then I hit him. Over and over. I wasn't thinking. I just needed to feel something.

Afterwards, when the noise died down, I looked at my hands. They were bloody, sweating and shaking. That's when I realised something about myself that scared me: **I loved violence.** I loved the way it made me feel. The rush, the control, the instant power. The pain was part of it too. It was like sex to me. Maybe better. I'd rather have a proper row than a night with anyone. The buzz of it, the explosion of it. No orgasm could touch that. I didn't know how to release pain any other way. I didn't know how to cry, how to talk, how to let it out and I didn't remember how to masturbate. So, I fought. I used my fists.

But violence can't fill you forever

5. SENTENCED

Standing in court that day, I remember the noise first, the scrape of shoes on the floor, the rustle of papers, the low hum of voices that never stopped. Fifteen of us stood there in total. Fifteen lads, all faces I knew from the streets, from the pubs, from the football grounds. We were all getting sentenced that morning.

The judge made a point of looking us over like we were a single body, a single problem that needed solving. His voice carried that tone, not angry, not emotional, just cold and deliberate. *"We are sending a message,"* he said. *"This kind of behaviour will not continue in Shropshire."*

He meant us. We were the message.

The five who stood closest to me were all in for the same kind of thing. Football violence, fights, affray, and the rest had their own charges: drugs, theft, assaults. Some worse than others. It didn't matter, because that day, we all felt the same weight pressing down. The Shropshire stratum, they called it. A clean-up job. They wanted to make an example of us.

When my name was called, I remember how my stomach dropped. The judge said, *"Twenty-two months"* like he was ordering coffee. Then he moved straight on to the next lad. I'd just left school six weeks earlier. I was still technically a kid, but that didn't matter in there. The system had already decided I was old enough to be punished like a man.

I still had other charges hanging over me. Sixteen months on another, some dropped, others pending. Altogether, I'd end up serving around two and a half years. But by then, I already knew what prison felt like. I'd done three months on remand before. I'd been in and out for six months in total. So, when they led me down that hallway, when the door slammed shut behind me, I didn't feel panic. It probably sounds strange to some people, but I felt *comfortable.* Not happy. Just familiar.

It was like going back to a place where, for once, the rules were clear.

No guessing. No pretending. Everyone knew where they stood. They sent me back to Stoke Heath, the same place I'd been on remand. As soon as I got there, I started seeing familiar faces. Some of the lads were still serving time. A few even called my name as I walked past, *"Magic!"* It was like we were back on the outside.

At first, I was put on D Wing; that's the remand wing and later moved to A Wing, middle landing. That was where the real mix was, young offenders, hardened criminals, the lifers who'd been there long enough to see the walls change colour.

Because I'd been inside before, I already knew how to move. I made acquaintances, built a few friendships, kept my head down but my eyes open.

The people I gravitated toward weren't small-time lads; they were serious people. Murderers. Drug dealers. Armed robbers. Football hooligans. Some of them were the same lads I'd fought against in Shrewsbury during matches against Wrexham. Strange how enemies can turn into *bredrins* once the walls close in.

The gangsters I mixed with came from everywhere, Birmingham, Manchester, and London. Some were B21 lads, heavy gangsters and known names from Birmingham. One of them introduced me to a man from a well-known Manchester family. His name had to be changed when he came in, because of who his people were. That was the company I found myself in.

We grew close in that strange *prison way*. You eat together, train together, survive together, and it becomes family. They taught me things I'd never known about myself, about my heritage, about being Jamaican and part Indian. They'd ask me:

"Why don't you like your own skin, Magic?"

"Why'd you fight for a football club that would never stand by a black lad?"

At first, I brushed it off. I didn't want to hear it. But they kept talking, and after a while, it sank in. They were right. I'd spent half my life trying to belong to people who'd never really wanted me there.

Inside, I saw plenty of fights. Some were quick and quiet, others loud and bloody. You learn fast when to look away and when to step in. I got caught in a few myself, but I was lucky. I had protection. The lads I was tight with ran that wing in their own way, so if anyone came for me, there'd be ten more ready to step in. You learn about loyalty in prison.

Some of those lads are still inside now. I speak to a couple even today. One found religion. Calls me now and again, tells me about peace and forgiveness. He's different now, and I respect that. Another one's still in, still living that life. You never really lose touch with the people who got you through those walls.

Because of my reputation, the staff treated me differently too. I wasn't a troublemaker, but I wasn't soft either. So, I got the best of what there was, better clothes when we swapped gear, better pad assignments, little privileges. When they gave awards for the cleanest cell or best work area, I was always in the mix. Little victories that made the time move faster.

There were other things too, things that never make the papers, although some of these escapades have hit the headlines recently. There were prison officers who crossed lines, favours traded for silence. Everyone knew, but no one talked. It was its own world, and the outside rules didn't apply.

Teachers used to tell me I'd get nowhere in life. They said it like it was a fact, not an opinion. I spent a lot of time in education, even though at first I didn't want to. I'd sit there pretending not to care, doodling on paper, watching the clock.

One day they gave us this test: some kind of science thing. I half-arsed my way through it, ticking boxes, not thinking much. When the results came back, they told me I scored 98%. Then, one teacher pulled me to the side after class. I thought I was in trouble again. He started talking about that test I'd done, the one I got 98% on. I thought he was taking the piss. But he said, "No, this wasn't just a science test; it was a psychology test. You should look into it when you get out."

That stuck with me because no one had ever said anything like that before. No one had ever said I had potential. Not my teachers outside, not the people at home. That word hit differently, *potential*. I didn't know what to do with it, but I carried it around in my head after that.

There were things in prison that didn't make sense. Like how they used to leave the young, vulnerable ones, the VPs, we called them, on the same landings as us. Everyone knew what some of them were in for. We didn't even need to be told. News travels fast inside. When we found out they were in for sexual stuff, the whole vibe changed.

We had our own rules in there. If you touched kids, you paid for it. That was the code. I know it sounds rough, but that's the way it was. I believed in that saying, *an eye for an eye, a tooth for a tooth*. Still do, in some ways.

I worked on the server, so I was the one handing out food; breakfast, dinner, all of it. The VPs used to come down later for their meals. We made sure they knew what we thought of them. Sometimes we'd do things to their food. I'm not gonna pretend it was right, but back then it felt right. It felt like we were doing something fair in an unfair place.

Do I regret it? Maybe not. Maybe a little. I just know at the time, I didn't feel bad about it. Not one bit. Bullying was a daily thing inside. It wasn't always about what you'd done; sometimes it was about how you looked, what shoes you wore, who you spoke to. People would test you for fun. You had to stand your ground, even when you were scared. If you showed weakness once, that was it; everyone tried you after that. I learned to stay firm. Keep your chin up. Keep your eyes open. Don't let anyone see fear. That was my survival.

Drugs were always about. The smell of spice, the staleness of smoke, it hung in the air like damp. People would trade anything for a hit. Food, clothes, favours. You could see it in their eyes, that dull glaze, the drift.

Prison was its own world. It had its own rules, its own system. It taught you structure, but it also fed the chaos in you. And once you got used to that chaos, being calm started to feel strange. We used to make hooch inside, proper *jail brew*. You'd use fruit, sugar, bread, whatever you could get your hands on. Leave it by the radiator, and after a few days it'd start bubbling. It stank, but it did the job. A few sips and the place felt lighter for a bit.

Weed and cannabis got sent in too. There was always someone on the outside who knew how to get it through. When the lights went out, we'd send lines under the pads, bits of string with a hook, to pass stuff from one cell to another. Everyone had their network. But if you didn't have a name, if people didn't rate you, you got nothing. That was the rule.

Cigarettes were still a big thing back then. Everyone smoked. You could smell it down the whole landing, that thick, heavy smoke that got into your clothes and stayed there. Mobile phones weren't around like they are now. I was inside from 2003 to 2005, and phones were still a luxury, not something everyone had tucked away. You wanted to get a message out; you passed it through word of mouth or through the lines.

You'd hear about stabbings now and then. Sometimes rumours, sometimes real. People going down over debt or pride. I never saw one happen in front of me, but I saw what it looked like after. Blood stains on the floor. Doors locked down. Everyone quiet for a while, then back to normal, like nothing happened. That's how it went, chaos followed by calm.

The worst part was the suicides. You'd wake up to whispers, "Someone's gone." It was always someone who'd been quiet, kept to themselves. You'd see their pad taped off, officers walking past with that look. Stoke Heath was a dark place in those days. You could feel it in the air. It got into your head if you let it.

But here's the thing I always tell young people when I talk to them now. I actually enjoyed my time inside. Sounds mad, I know, but it's true. I went in with the mindset of *I don't give a shit*. I wasn't scared. I'd already been through worse on the outside. Prison gave me time to think.

Inside, I learned more about who I was than I ever had out there. I learned about my roots; my Jamaican side and my Indian side things no one ever told me about before. I started understanding where I came from, why I'd felt so lost for so long. But it wasn't all good learning. Along with that came the bad stuff, new tricks, new street knowledge, new ways to hustle. You learn crime quicker than you learn anything else in a place like that.

6. STUCK IN THE CYCLE

When I left prison, my mom was there waiting at the gates. I'll never forget that moment. The air felt fresh, but strange, like the world had been moving on without me and I was stepping back into it too fast. She stood by the car holding a small bag of clothes she'd brought for my birthday. I'd turned eighteen inside, and she said she didn't want me walking out in prison greys.

She handed me the bag, a pair of jeans, a shirt, and trainers, simple stuff, but to me it felt like gold. I remember touching the fabric, just the feel of real clothes, and for a second I was happy. Proper happy. But underneath that, I was gutted. I was on bail for something that had happened inside, so I knew things weren't exactly free yet. And worse, I already knew I wasn't going home. She visited me the week before and told me straight:

"You're not coming back to live with me."

I'd nodded like I understood, but inside I felt sick. So, when I saw her outside the gates, I had all these mixed feelings banging around in my head, happy to see her, happy to be out, but already knowing what was waiting for me would not be easy.

She hugged me, said she was proud of me for "keeping my head down," but her eyes told a different story, tired, guarded, like she was saying goodbye as much as hello.

We drove off in silence for a bit. The world outside looked louder, brighter, too fast. Freedom didn't feel like freedom; it felt like stepping into somewhere you didn't belong anymore. We got in the car and went for breakfast. I hadn't sat in a cafe in years, so the smell of fried bacon, burnt toast, and coffee hit me straight away. Everything felt loud: the sound of plates clattering, people laughing, normal life happening around me. I sat there in my prison-issue coat, still half in another world.

Mum sat across from me, stirring her tea, quiet for a bit. Then she said, "Here's £200 from your post office account. Go fend for yourself."

That was it. No plan, no "come and stay with me, "nothing. I was homeless. Just like that. I didn't argue. I didn't have the energy to. She handed me the money, and I just nodded. We ate in silence, and when we finished, she hugged me once outside, said, "Look after yourself," and drove off.

I stood there watching her car disappear down the road. That's when it hit me. I was free, but I had nowhere to go.

The first thing I did was go for a drink. I ended up in this pub in Shrewsbury that's not even there anymore. I blew through the money on booze. Rounds for me, rounds for anyone who'd listen. I just wanted to feel something other than empty. I'd been given my freedom, but it didn't feel like freedom; it felt like being dropped into the world with no map.

I still had some money left from my canteen account, about £275.03 in total. I remember the exact number. That was everything I owned in the world. The next day I went to the job centre, tried to sign on. Sat in a line of people waiting for help, the smell of damp coats and old carpet, everyone looking half asleep. When it was my turn, the woman behind the desk asked about my work history. I didn't have one. She asked about the gaps. I told her the truth: *I'd been inside.* You could see the light change in her eyes. One second polite, the next cautious. That's when I realised how hard it was gonna be. No one wanted to give a lad like me a chance.

So, I did what I knew. I went back to selling. Drugs were easy money, and I was good at it. It wasn't smart, but it was survival. The streets didn't care about your CV; that wasn't important. They cared if you could handle yourself, and I could.

But it didn't take long for trouble to find me again. I ran into issues with my ex and her crowd, and one night at The Rock and Fountain, one of the main pubs back then, I got jumped by five of the top lads. Proper top lads, older than me. They tried to put me down quick. I remember the noise, the fists, boots, shouts, all of it blurring together. I hit the ground hard, but I stood back up. Blood in my mouth, lip split, head spinning. I spat the blood out, right at them, and said, "Is that all you can do to an eighteen-year-old?" They didn't expect that. They froze. That's when I knew I wasn't beaten.

After that, there weren't any more issues, not directly. But the truth is, being black in that scene was always an issue. Didn't matter if you were loyal, if you fought for the same club, or stood shoulder to shoulder. I was still the black lad in a world that didn't want me in it. And because I wouldn't leave my girlfriend, who was white, some people made sure I paid for it. The more the pressure built, the deeper I went back into crime and drugs. It became my way of coping. Looking back now, I know how lucky I am to be writing this book. Because if I'd been caught for some things I did back then, and I mean really caught, I'd be inside for life.

For about two months I lived in a pub, scraping together whatever I could. At that time my grandad was caring for my nan. She'd had bacterial meningitis, was bed-bound and in a wheelchair, and the illness left her with brain damage. My grandad couldn't bear to see me like a stranger: practically homeless in a B&B, he brought me into their home. God bless them. I wish I'd treated them better.

I tried to contribute. I'd give my grandad money for the house and he'd always ask where it came from. He had his suspicions: people would come to the door, shout through the windows. Once a group gathered outside; I grabbed a knife, went out, and pulled one lad aside by the neck, telling him to shut up, after all this was my grandparents' home. I was hardly ever there. I'd disappear on Wednesday and maybe not come back until Sunday, if I needed to. I'd leave again on Sunday night. I was in and out, living two lives under the same roof.

It was while I was living this way that I met my childhood sweetheart. We spent three years together and got engaged. But it didn't last because she cheated and we broke up. I spiralled. I planned revenge. I imagined violence as the answer. The plan never came to pass because I went out the night before and we picked up a huge stash of drugs. We always bought on certain days. On a Tuesday or a Wednesday, and that night we picked so much that the next few days blurred into one long, drugged haze.

By then I had drug runners, who sold for me so I didn't have to shift the product myself. I wasn't just using drugs; I was dealing too; I was at the centre of it all. My body and mind were wrecked. I'd gone from thirteen stone when I left prison to nine stone in about three months. I was taking steroids and cocaine, a terrible cocktail. I was a furious man. I'd knocked out a bouncer outside a club, carried knives, and had several run-ins because the rage was always close to the surface.

While I was collapsing into that week of benders, I lost people who mattered. One of my best friends died after an epileptic fit not long after getting out of prison. An ex-girlfriend had also died from an overdose. Those deaths should have been wake-up calls. Instead, I spent days at my mate's flat taking every drug there was and drinking until time stopped. When I finally rang one of my runners, he shouted, "Where the fuck have you been?" I thought it was the same day, but he told me I'd been sanctioned for seven days. My supply had been taken away. I'd been cut off.

I was taken back to my grandparents. I stayed a few days, barely eating. My mum saw me and said, "Look at the state of you." For the first time, she made a decision I never thought she would make. Mum sent me to my *sperm donor*. My sperm donor had been cut off from us for years. He was on the run and involved in serious violent crime. For my mum to put me on a ferry to meet him in Holyhead, Ireland, showed how desperate she was. When I finally met my sperm donor properly, the first thing I asked one of his friends for was cocaine. My sperm donor found out, he was livid and he grabbed me. In that moment I realised how low I'd sunk.

There are stories from Ireland I could tell forever. Spending time with my siblings, learning the culture, feeling the warmth of people who weren't wrapped up in the same violence and drugs. Irland helped me breathe for a while. But even on the border, things weren't clean. Gangs existed there, too. I saw fights, bouncers stabbed, cars set on fire. There were pubs I couldn't enter because of the IRA. A drive-by happened near my sperm donor's house while I'd been out. One morning I woke to Garda everywhere. They told us the house had been threatened because of drug allegations. Still, I cherished the months I spent with my sperm donor and siblings. I didn't come back a different man, but I returned with a colder outlook on relationships and a little more distance from my old self.

Back in Shrewsbury, the trouble didn't end. I had a falling-out with a lad who'd been a friend. He hit me over a cheating scandal, and I didn't let things lie. Months later I planned to go after him, I carried masks, machetes, knives. I drove around town with mates, turned up at his ex's house; they saw me and spotted my tattoo and called my name, and we left. Time passed. We eventually sorted things out and, strangely, became close again in prison. He was one of the few I respected. Then he was murdered by people we both knew. He was stabbed eight times. His murder hit me hard. I could have been the one who did it if my earlier plan had worked. Even though we'd reconciled, I felt powerless and guilty.

The losses piled up. My grandad died around the same time. My cousin hung himself in prison. He'd been held on gun charges. The country felt unsustainable, full of dead ends and bad choices.

So, I bought a one-way ticket to Thailand.

At first it felt like escape. I thought I'd stay with a friend, but he left soon after. I stayed in Thailand for three months, met bright people with easy smiles, and fell in love with the heat and the sounds, the birds, the buzz of markets, the nights that smelled of spice. There was ugliness too: racism in small pockets, gangs, and people who made money off others in the worst ways. I moved on to Cambodia. For a short time, I even taught English at an orphanage, untrained, swearing a lot, but it meant something. Handing out pens and notepads, walking into classrooms and connecting with kids who had so little, that was one of the truest moments I've had. It made me appreciate that, despite everything, I hadn't grown up in an orphanage. It humbled me.

But the dark parts followed. In Southeast Asia, I drank and took synthetic drugs. Mcat was brutal. There were nights I couldn't remember, situations I can't explain. At times a friend from home tried to sell his girlfriend; the things I saw made my skin crawl. Running away had solved nothing.

I pulled myself away and stayed with my aunt for a while. For four months I laid off the worst of it. I ran every day, ate properly, cut down on the drinking, only having a beer here and there. I met my future ex-wife just before I was due to join the armed forces. For the first time in a long while, something felt possible. The future was, for a moment, quieter and straighter. I'd traded the pubs and the drugs for running shoes and drills, and it felt like a chance (maybe the first real one) to stop drifting.

7. SEX & DRUGS

Eventually, it burned itself out, or maybe I did. When I stopped fighting. When I stopped moving like I was made of fire, my body rebelled. The violence had been my release valve, and once it was gone, something inside me ruptured. The seizures started without warning. My whole body would lock and thrash as if all the years of chaos had been stored under my skin, waiting for a crack to break through. The doctors told me it was drug-induced epilepsy. I didn't argue. It felt like my body had been fighting a war I didn't even know I'd enlisted in. I couldn't fight anymore, so my body fought for me.

That's when drugs took over completely. They replaced the violence. They became the new language of survival, one high at a time.

Always weed first. The weed softened the edges, turned the noise down just enough so I could breathe. It was the closest thing I had to comfort. A daily thing, a ritual, like lighting a candle in a dark room. But soft things never lasted long in my life. Weed was only ever the doorway. Once the numbness got familiar, I wanted something stronger, harder, something that didn't just take the pain away but erased the entire shape of it.

Speed came next. Pink powder folded into a Rizla, the so-called base. I can still taste it, the bitter chemical sting at the back of my throat, the electric jolt beneath my skin. The first time was at the bus stop by the marsh. We stood there all night, talking nonsense like it mattered, watching the sky fade from black to grey. Speed warped time. It stretched moments until they snapped. Midnight turned into morning without warning, the milkman rolling past, birds starting their shift. Sixteen hours vanished, and I was still wired, still buzzing, like my bones were vibrating under my skin. My head felt clear, painfully clear, like every thought had razor edges.

Then came E. Those pills hit completely differently. Where speed made me sharp and scattered, E made everything soft and connected. It rewired my brain temporarily. Made me feel like I wasn't a single person locked inside a skull but part of something bigger. I'd look at my mates and swear we were communicating without speaking. Music felt cleaner; lights breathed. My chest loosened for the first time in years. It tricked me into thinking I wasn't alone.

And then cocaine, the one that pretended to be the answer to everything. Coke made me feel like a god. It wrapped confidence around me like armour. I could talk faster, move faster, think faster. I felt untouchable. It gave me the illusion of control, the illusion that I was finally someone worth noticing. And when I started selling it, the feeling doubled. Money in my pocket, fresh clothes, people nodding at me with respect I'd never earned. I mistook that for happiness.

But Coke is a liar. It gives and then it takes. The highs became shorter. The come downs hit harder. The confidence twisted into paranoia. Every shadow felt like a threat. Every silence felt like an accusation. Sometimes I'd lie there staring at the ceiling, heart pounding, convinced something was watching me from inside my own skull. I knew I was sinking, but the moment I could stand again, I'd go straight back to it. Coke was control and chaos in the same breath.

Weed numbed the pain. Coke magnified it. Speed stretched time until it lost meaning. E. erased the loneliness for a few hours. Every drug did something different to me, but all of them worked together like gears in a machine I couldn't switch off.

All of it became my new way of coping.

And deep down, I think I always knew: the drugs were doing exactly what the violence used to. Keeping me alive while slowly killing me.

I was sexually aware at eight or nine, I would look under the tables up the girls' skirts. I was excessively for my age, curious about bodies, both male and female, but especially girls. I was interested in sexual body parts. I used to masturbate a lot; it was an innate drive, and it was my release of tension. My counsellor said that I shouldn't have known these things at that age but we never uncovered whether I was actually sexually abused as a child.

That sexual drive was further fuelled by drugs. As I got older, I got involved in swinging in my late teens/ early twenties. I was sexually experienced with girls but then, when drugs took over my life, I was introduced to orgies, anything, and everything went, male and female combined. It wasn't a secret; it was part of the life, all kinds of sex with multiple partners. I am not gay, but in my teens I questioned my sexuality, especially when I took ecstasy. Thoughts of same-sex acts came to my mind but I never acted on them. I didn't like the thoughts. It was the drugs.

Cocaine made me feel like a super sexy stud. It is a huge sexual liberator; I lost all my inhibitions. All of my relationships with women were highly sexually charged. I got heavily into swinging; I joined the sites and got involved; I was promiscuous, and I would wake up in an orgy and think, *what the fuck am I doing?* And I would leave. I had a vague recollection of what happened, but not all the others involved remembered bits to so we would try to piece it together, but our memories were clouded by the comedown from the drugs. I was on and off the swinging website in my twenties and into my thirties; I was into swinging but I fucking hated it! I hated it then and I hate it now; it made me feel dirty; I didn't like what I was doing. Now I just think it was all part of me finding who I was, my identity and belonging.

We did some crazy things back then; I took crack, crystal meth, and MCAT. One time, me and my mate went

Mushroom picking in Gains Park In Shrewsbury. We had gone to a mental health hospital, formerly known as Shelton Hospital, but it was being demolished. I think it was haunted; we were off our heads, and we took a walking stick we found back with us. I felt a bad energy from it, maybe because of the drugs. Anyway, we then walked back and picked up a milk carton off a doorstep and started drawing weird sexual stuff on it. We left the carton there. Then about 5 months later, when I was In phase one training in the army, I got a phone call from the police. I was surprised as I hadn't been in any sort of trouble for a while. Apparently, there was a report made to the police by the man whose doorstep the milk was on about provocative images on his milk. The man was in witness protection and he was worried the criminals had found him. The desk sergeant was laughing about it but it really wasn't that funny.

Another part of the world we were in was selling women; well, we tried to. There was a girl I knew in Monksmoor and she agreed for me and another dealer to sell her for sex in Manchester. It was agreed but it never happened. Not something I am proud of but it was all part of that world.

8. LIFE IN THE ARMY

I didn't join the Army to fight for the Queen (now the King). I joined because I needed discipline. I knew that if I didn't take control of my life, I would end up dead or back in prison. It took seven years to get in: five years waiting for my convictions to be spent, and another two because I had been prescribed antidepressants. When I tried joining earlier, they told me to wait. I stuck with it because I'd promised myself I would make it.

My mum's voice was always in the back of my head, telling me I'd never join. That became fuel. I needed to prove her wrong.

Phase 1 training in Winchester was a shock to the system. I went in at 14½ stone and left at 10½. The physical demands were brutal, but the mental strain was worse. I expected to struggle with authority, and there were times I confronted sergeants who got in my face. During icebreakers, people were stunned by my past, the violence, stabbings, drugs, death. One sergeant said I sounded like I'd lived a life equivalent to a deployment in Afghanistan.

Being older helped me. At 28, with more life experience than most recruits, the lads looked up to me. Despite the rough edges, I enjoyed parts of Phase 1. It broke me down and built me up in ways I hadn't expected.

Phase 2 brought more freedom. I'd proposed to my then-girlfriend during my Passing Out parade, a public moment in front of family and friends. After three weeks' leave, I began Phase 2. There were more nights out and more chances to meet people who came from similar backgrounds.

Training was constant: running, military tests, driving lessons. I passed everything. Yet emotionally, Phase 2 was harder to grasp. It felt like a limbo between who I had been and who I was trying to become.

After Phase 2, we married and I joined my regiment in Tidworth. The distance between Wales and Tidworth, three to four hours, was the first real strain. Regiment life had its own problems. The saying is true: if your face doesn't fit, you won't feel welcomed. Racism wasn't always overt, but it showed in the roles people were given. I saw talented African soldiers stuck in lower ranks. It made the environment tense.

The drinking culture dominated everything. People drank daily, and that lifestyle seeped into my marriage. Arguments over alcohol were constant. I sensed something wasn't right at home but couldn't prove it. Later I discovered that a mate of mine had been spending hours at my ex-wife's house telling no one. Whether they had an affair, the secrecy was enough to break me.

Belgium was the turning point. My marriage was cracking, I was under counselling for depression, and my stability was hanging by a thread. I wasn't meant to be deployed, but they sent me anyway. I was just a number they needed filled.

My first epileptic fit happened there. One moment I was upright; the next I woke on the floor, surrounded by medics and shouting voices. My body had betrayed me publicly, limbs jerking, jaw locked, the confusion like a fog I couldn't shake.

The second fit came during gym instructor training. I remember the metallic taste in my mouth before everything snapped away. When I opened my eyes, lads were trying to steady me, calling for help.

The third seizure was the worst. I was on the phone to my best mate. My words turned to gibberish mid-sentence — he thought I was drunk. I dropped the phone, collapsed, hit my head, and woke to a diagnosis: **juvenile myoclonic epilepsy**. When they asked if I'd had seizures before, I told them about the drug-induced episodes from years earlier. My past and my present had collided.

The truth was simple: I shouldn't have been deployed. I'd been classed as depressed and under counselling, but they flew me to Belgium anyway. My breakdown played out in front of the regiment, violent and humiliating. I even explored legal action. Nothing came of it.

Those seizures marked the beginning of the end. My body had cracked. My mind followed.

When everything came out about my marriage, and with my health in ruins, I lost control. I went AWOL for a week. I flipped a car with people inside. We could have all died. I got into fights. I sliced someone's face. The Army was full of violence, drugs, trafficking, and alcohol. I'd joined to escape that life and somehow ended up surrounded by it again.

The only time I found real stability was during my resettlement course. For 12 months I had one job: prepare for civilian life. I wanted to finish my personal training qualifications and work with young people. Because I was classed as injured because of epilepsy, I received good support. I didn't like the label, but I needed the help.

Resettlement brought genuine positivity. I did The Prince's Trust Team Leading Course. I stayed in Crewe for a week for training, hotel, classes, meeting good people. They lined up a job for me in Stafford as a Prince's Trust Team Leader. I finished my PT qualifications and formed real friendships, including one friend who brought me into her family and supported me during the darkest period of my life.

For the first time, I saw what a healthy environment looked like, people who were kind wanting nothing from me. It was eye-opening. My resettlement matured me more than my Army service ever had.

At Tidworth House, I also began training for the Invictus Games. I met Lewis Hamilton and several footballers. I saw veterans of extraordinary strength and resilience. I felt out of place, like I didn't deserve to be among them, but their kindness stayed with me. From that moment, I felt a need to give something back, to repay what I'd been given.

My Army years were a mixture of discipline, chaos, opportunity, and collapse. But the final year, the year of rebuilding, was where the real change happened. I left with qualifications, direction, and the determination to help young people avoid the mistakes I made.

The Army didn't save me, but it gave me enough tools to start saving myself.

9. TRYING TO REBUILD

When I left the Armed Forces, I joined the Prince's Trust for six months. I knew I needed help with my mental health. I was already on a waiting list for counselling. Because of my epilepsy and a drink-driving conviction from when I was in the Army, I couldn't drive. So, every morning I walked 45 minutes from my house to the train station, then another three miles from Stafford station to the fire station where I worked. I did that journey in rain, heat, and frost every day for six months.

Staffordshire Fire Service eventually offered me a permanent job with the Prince's Trust. I loved it. I still have the certificate they gave me, framed on my wall. That role opened the door to youth work: kids from every background, every faith, every story. The building always smelled faintly of smoke and polish; the corridors echoed with young voices and the thud of boots. It felt warm, familiar. For the first time in years, I felt like I belonged somewhere.

I was also volunteering during that time. The woman who ran the project is now Godmother to my daughter. She was one of the first people to believe in me completely.

But the travel took its toll. In summer, the heat made the long walks bearable, even peaceful. In winter, the cold cut through my coat and froze my breath. My legs ached constantly and the dark mornings made the journey feel endless. Eventually, I realised I needed something closer to home.

I started working at a youth care home and stayed for about four years. I met so many young people with stories heavier than most adults could handle. One lad I mentored now calls me his dad or older brother. I'm Godfather to his son. We still speak every day. I believed in him when others wrote him off.

But inside the care system, I saw things that angered me. Some staff were only there for the money. Senior staff openly said they didn't like the kids. Hearing people in positions of responsibility dismiss vulnerable young people made my blood boil. I worked overtime constantly, sometimes three or four days on instead of the usual two. Partly for the kids, partly because my home life was falling apart and work became an escape.

Despite my commitment, despite press cuttings on the walls showing my achievements, I was never promoted. For years I did the job of an assistant manager or team leader while being paid the same low wage.

Around that time, I began building my own organisation: **New Generation Coaching**. My ex-partner encouraged me to take the idea seriously. But life was overflowing. I was working seven days a week, going to counselling, running my organisation, and dealing daily with young people telling me traumatic stories.

Counselling opened up a can of worms inside me. I had unresolved trauma and childhood pain I'd never processed. And I didn't handle it well. I perpetrated domestic violence, something I take full responsibility for. It is a mistake that changed my life and one I carry with me. I was arrested for assault and criminal damage, though the charges were later dropped. I felt relief, but also deep shame. My family didn't deserve any of it. My daughter didn't deserve to be kept from me for months. That was my doing.

During this time, I started drinking heavily without fully understanding why. I had everything in front of me and was destroying it piece by piece. I was unravelling.

A young person disclosed something horrific from his childhood. It scarred me and I didn't cope. I was caught drinking at work and lost my job. After four years of dedication, no promotion, no support, I was dismissed for gross misconduct.

My relationship collapsed. Days later I crashed my car. Then COVID hit. My organisation almost collapsed. The DBS sent a letter saying they might bar me from working with young people. I felt dirty, like I'd been labelled something I wasn't. I had to ask people I worked with — teachers, youth workers, kids themselves to write statements for me. In the end, I received a No-Action letter, but the process broke me. Sixty references came in. I was grateful, but I was exhausted.

During COVID I had no job, no income except Universal Credit, no routine. I couldn't see my daughter for three months. The house was too quiet. My children's photos stared at me from the walls, each one pulling me deeper into guilt. I began self-harming. I attempted suicide. My friend walked in and found me hanging from a curtain rail. It wasn't a cry for help...he simply walked in at the exact moment I was slipping away.

After that, I spiralled. A friend involved in drug dealing had money to collect, six figures. We bought a shotgun and argued about cutting the barrel. Crime felt like an easy escape, a familiar road.

Then, my phone buzzed.

An email.

I opened it and saw I'd been **nominated for a Positive Role Model Award**. Comments from teachers, parents, young people. Pages of people saying how much I'd helped them, how I'd changed their lives. Reading their words was like cold water across my face. I felt ashamed, ashamed that I was about to throw everything away.

It was a penny-drop moment. I told my mate, "I can't fucking do this." And I walked away.

The landlady from Cardiff, someone who had become like family, told me to come and stay. I took the train during lockdown, past police watching the station gates. Cardiff felt different: the air smelled of sea and wet pavements; gulls cried overhead; the quiet streets echoed under lockdown rules.

I stayed there for months. We had BBQs in the back garden. We took long walks along the river. I reduced the drinking, stopped the drugs, and focused on myself. I went through old emails and comments from people who believed in me. For the first time in a long while, I saw the good I had done. It grounded me.

But mentally, I was still battling. Depression, anxiety, epilepsy, and a recent autism diagnosis hit me all at once. When I returned home, I felt frustrated and angry; I felt like, if schools had known about my ADHD and ASD earlier, I might have been supported differently, maybe even lived differently.

I continued to struggle with suicidal thoughts. Medication helped, but the fight remained. Some days I couldn't leave the house. Some days the world felt too heavy. But friends and a few family members kept me going.

My daughter's mother and I tried to fix things, but it didn't work. Still, I began getting work again through New Generation Coaching. The No-Action letter cleared me. Telford Council confusion caused setbacks, but eventually I was allowed back into schools. For two years

MISUNDERSTOOD

I mentored young people and supported outreach at my old school. Slowly, things looked better.

I wasn't healed. But I was moving.

10. WHAT'S EFFING WRONG WITH ME?

Loads of my mates have managed to build long-term relationships, settled, stable, growing old with someone. Meanwhile, I've been bouncing through about fifteen relationships. Some lasted months, some half a year, maybe a year if things didn't completely fall apart. My longest one has stretched to six years, on and off. I'm nearly 39 now, and somehow love and relationships have never stuck for me, maybe this time.

After a while, I started asking myself the question that kept me up at night: **"What's fucking wrong with me?"** I used to fall in love so fast it felt like free-fall. Head over heels, feelings coming in strong before I even had a chance to slow them down. I romanticised everything, wanted that deep connection, that one person I could actually trust.

But every time, I ended up hurt, cheated on, lied to, used, discarded. It didn't matter how good my intentions were; the ending was always the same.

And I wasn't innocent. I had a reputation for violence on the streets, in arguments, as a way of expressing myself. That anger leaked into relationships sometimes. I didn't know how to talk about my feelings, how to be vulnerable without feeling weak. Relationships felt like a test I never studied for, and the only tools I had were the wrong ones. I was self-medicating with drugs, booze, chaos... anything to calm the storms in my head. These crutches held me up just long enough for me to keep falling again.

Underneath, though, there was always this ache, this heavy unhappiness. I wanted love. Proper love. I wanted someone who'd stay, someone I could build a life with. But every time I reached for that, all I got was pain.

After enough heartbreaks, something in me hardened. I stopped giving my heart away so easily. I told myself that being nice didn't work. You just got walked over. So, I slipped into that mindset: treat them mean, keep them keen. Act cold, stay distant, don't show too much. It wasn't who I was, not really, but it felt safer than being the guy who loved too much and got destroyed for it.

Eventually, I realised I couldn't keep pretending my behaviour, past, or present, existed in a vacuum. I needed answers. I needed to understand myself. So I went through therapy, treatment, assessments... years of digging through the mess I'd been carrying. That's when everything started making sense. I was diagnosed with bulimia nervosa; I'd been bingeing and purging for years without connecting the dots. Then, Autism Spectrum Disorder, epilepsy, anxiety, depression, and Combined ADHD. A whole mix of things I'd been living with blind.

Not knowing about these conditions affected everything; how I loved, how I communicated, how I dealt with anger, fear, disappointment. They shaped every relationship I ever stepped into. It's not an excuse for the harm I caused or the choices I made. It's more like finally realising that I wasn't just "broken". I was misunderstood, even by myself.

Now, I'm learning acceptance and it feels like the foundation of something real.

11. WHERE I AM NOW & MY FUTURE ASPIRATIONS

After everything that happened, life finally settled. I found work at a company completely different from anything I'd done before. I made a conscious decision to avoid the care system. Listening to traumatic stories from young people seven days a week had taken a serious toll on my mental health, and I knew I needed to protect myself. After being rejected from roles in youth care because of my past, I took a step back and rebuilt from a distance.

So, where am I now?

2020 was one of the hardest years of my life. My relationship broke down. I was caught drink-driving again. I attempted suicide once by stabbing my leg with a kitchen knife, once by trying to hang myself. Over Christmas, the police broke down my door to check if I was still alive. That same holiday season, I overdosed on medication. It felt like everything was collapsing around me.

But something shifted. I was diagnosed with ADHD, and suddenly a lot of my past made sense — the chaos, the impulsivity, the extreme highs and lows. That diagnosis gave me clarity I'd never had before. Now, when I speak to young people, I tell them to get help early. Don't wait decades. Don't carry your pain alone.

Despite everything, bright moments emerged. Over the past four years I've been nominated for **three National Diversity Awards**. In 2024, I received three new nominations. I was even featured in a musical production about *The Drifters*. I still work with young people, and now also support adults battling addiction, helping them get into employment and regain control of their lives.

I'm writing this book because I want the story out there, and one day, I want it made into a film. It's been a rollercoaster life: intense highs, crushing lows, many driven by ADHD, many caused by my own decisions. I've been misunderstood, unsupported, and unprepared at different stages, as a child, in relationships, and in work environments. But I kept moving. I held on.

I take responsibility for everything I've done, good and bad. I'm not pretending to be a saint. I've been violent. I've damaged relationships. I've caused hurt. But I've also been helped. The Prince's Trust, Help for Heroes, and the Royal British Legion carried me through some of my darkest moments. Last Christmas, after the police broke my door down, I faced huge energy bills and debt. Those organisations covered the cost of the new door, cut my electric bill, and gave me food vouchers. I'm grateful beyond words.

A lot of my outbursts came from not knowing how to talk about my emotions. I was a scared kid who couldn't express what was happening inside. And now, as a grown man, I still struggle. I still fear being called a liar. I still fear people pointing fingers instead of listening. There were times I didn't want to exist at all.

But I turned a corner.

Today, I have a simple life with my children. I'm happy. I'm working. I'm helping young people find paths I never had. Opportunities keep coming, doors keep opening, and my organisation, **New Generation Coaching** is growing because I refused to let anyone take it away from me.

My goal now is straightforward: I won't allow any young person I work with to feel the way I felt, unheard, misunderstood and alone. They deserve better. They deserve what I never had.

If you've read this far, thank you for walking with me through the chaos, the mistakes, the growth, and the healing.

From struggle to self.

God bless.

AFTERWORD

Since writing the first draft of this book, I was awarded the **BLAC Excellence Second Chance Achiever Award in October 2025**, a moment that still feels surreal. If you had told me years ago that someone with my past, someone once consumed by hatred and violence, would receive a BLAC award, I would never have believed it. The irony isn't lost on me: a former Neo-Nazi being honoured for positive impact and change.

A play has also been written and performed about my story, bringing parts of my life to the stage in a way I never imagined possible. And now, I am developing a documentary about my journey.

My past doesn't define who I am today, but it shapes the message I want to share. Transformation is possible, no matter how far gone you think you are.

'Some people will write me as a villain in their stories and portray me as such... but that is for their own gratification and self-belief that they are better than me... but it is them that are the villains. They brought out a side of me I never wanted or asked for but was part of my survival. Especially at a young age, when all I needed was love, nurture, and protection, and all I had was neglection, abuse and misunderstood!'

MISUNDERSTOOD

Now you have read my story, I invite you to view the trailer of my documentary.

This is the trailer for the documentary about my life:

The Black Skinhead.

A Recent Feature on BBC News

TESTIMONIALS AND ENDORSEMENTS.

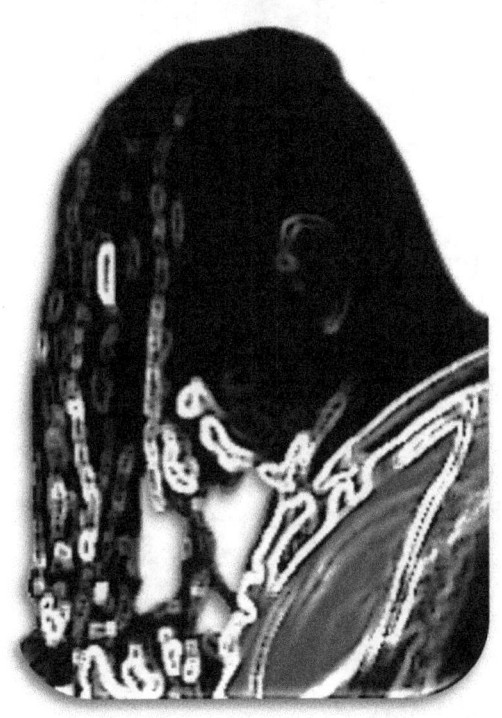

Thank you from young person

Key Worker Ben

I want say thank you to this lad he's helped me through alot of things like my beg weight loss he stood right next to me showing me the ways to go he helped me when i was down even stood by me when i was quite a horrible lad he never gave up he's a great individual I want that thank him for every thing hes done for me he may have been my key worker but i seen him as a best friend his personality just everything about him is great if i just moved into pemberton house i would choose him as my key worker no doubt about Cant thak you enough bro much love i have nothing but respect for you i wish you and your family well love you bro

Craig Walton — Social Worker

"The world of social work can feel a very small place especially when you are a social worker living in the same area where you work. This was the case for me during my early career when I worked in the field of child protection. This is when I first met Ben.

Although my primary focus was on child protection cases, I also addressed referrals concerning children deemed to be in need. It was under such circumstances that I visited Ben and his family in the early 2000s.

At that time, the police had been called to their home due to an incident, and there were growing concerns from his school about Ben's unstable living situation, as he was frequently staying with friends. Additionally, his behaviour raised alarms, particularly his connections with the English Border Front, a football hooligan group linked to Shrewsbury Town F.C. At the time of my referral, Ben's father was incarcerated, and he lived with his mother, stepfather, and younger brother. Ben would sometimes find solace at his grandparents' home in Shrewsbury, which often served as a refuge during difficult times at home. Ben was also sofa surfing at numerous friends in the area.

Concerns for Ben were present, but the issues did not meet the criteria for child protection intervention. Consequently, my time with Ben concluded as I needed to focus on children who were in greater need of safeguarding.

Ben was a young individual who seemed reluctant to share the realities of his home life or the dynamics of his local community. Despite several attempts to connect with him during our walks and coffee outings after school, my efforts to explore his experiences were consistently met with polite evasions. Although Ben was an engaging person, I sensed that he was grappling with deeper issues, and my concern for the direction he was heading grew. Unfortunately, without his trust and willingness to open up about his story, I had no choice but to close his referral, leaving the school to continue monitoring his situation closely.

I spent several more years working in child protection while remaining in the same community. During this time, I frequently encountered Ben in Shrewsbury Town Centre or at the local COOP. He was always his charming self, greeting me with a few friendly words and a wave whenever we crossed paths. Unfortunately, I was also aware that these encounters coincided with Ben's growing disillusionment with school, his involvement in risky criminal activities, and his deeper entanglement with the EBF.

I remember a few years later standing behind Ben at the local COOP, where he was purchasing a bottle of wine while I grabbed a few cans of beer. As he made his payment, I caught a glimpse of his army I.D. card and I felt relief. It felt like the army could be his refuge, offering him a chance to escape the demons of his past and sever the ties that had been dragging him into a life of drugs and crime.

Ben and I reconnected in his 30s, a time when I had established a fostering agency and he was working in residential care and knife prevention. True to his friendly and charming nature, Ben surprised me by sharing details about his early years. I couldn't help but wonder why he hadn't confided in me sooner; perhaps if he had, we could have altered the course of his life.

My experiences with Ben highlighted the vital role of relationships and the effort required to earn someone's trust. Trust is essential; without it, young people may hesitate to open up about their lives.

Ben deserves recognition for his ability to navigate life's challenges while also supporting others, guiding them away from the difficult paths he faced as a teenager. I would like to wish him every success with all his ventures.

Craig Walton, Social Worker.

Smid

"Let me introduce myself. I go by the name Smid, and around 2004 I got incarcerated. They sent me to an HMYOI prison, namely Stoke Heath. While doing my sentence I met a lot of young people my age, but only some really stood out in my mind. Benjamin Butler was one of them.

From my recollection, I started on A Wing, which was the induction wing at the time. Helps you get used to the rules and regulations. I got the ropes pretty quick, which resulted in me getting moved to main population. So, from there, straight to C Wing, where most of the stood lads had been in the jail a while.

The first cell I was put in was adjacent to Ben Butler's cell. We soon struck up our first convo, which started something like:

"Oi, Pad 8?"

Me, not knowing I'm Pad 8, didn't reply.

He shouted again: "Oiii, Pad 8!"

Once again, me not knowing I'm Pad 8, didn't reply. Then he said to another prisoner, "Bang his wall and shout 'Pad 8, why's he ignoring me?'"

Then I heard a thump on my wall. That's when I realised, shit, I must be Pad 8. So, I made my way to the door to chat through the gap. He asked where I was from. I told him. I asked where he was from. He told me. After that initial chat we had nothing else to say, so it was kinda like, "Chat to you on sosh"; which, for those who don't know, is association time: phones, pool, shower time.

As the days passed we used to chat more, get a feel for one another. Is he my type of person? Will we get along? Me and Ben were very different, from very different backgrounds, but we had so much in common.

I remember the first time I asked him what he was in for. He said, "I'm a football hooligan, I'm on a firm." I knew of football firms, but never really met anybody actually in one, so that was different and interesting.

But as we bonded and chatted more, I started to realise he's a very good guy. At the time, I didn't know much about his roots, and this is what we ended up bonding over a lot. I'm very proud of my heritage and skin colour, so I always used to let Ben know be proud of your white side, but bro, you will be seen as a coloured person no matter what—so you need to know and be proud of who you are. And it was something he was instantly interested in and proud to do.

When he'd talk about life outside prison, I could tell where he's from—majority white and a different world to what I'm used to. It made me realise it was good for Ben to meet people just like him, to understand who he really is.

Due to me always being down block, and Ben having a stint down block just before he was released, we weren't around each other as much toward the end. But by then we'd already formed a brotherhood and a lifelong friendship. We traded numbers toward the end.

The day he got out, I was heading down block for my adjudication, and Ben was just leaving the block. As we passed each other he was like, "Smiddy, I'm going home today." Inside I was a lil sad my bro was leaving, but at the same time so happy for him to get out of that shithole. We hugged, and I vowed, "Bro, don't worry, I'll ring you when I'm out." We both smiled and parted ways. That was the last time I saw Butler in jail.

BEN J. BUTLER

I kept my promise, and on the day I was released I rang Ben on his mum's home number. She answered and asked who it was. I said, "His friend from jail. Tell him Smid." From the icy response I got, I wondered if she'd pass the message on. I never heard from Ben again.

I thought about him over the years—who he's become, if he's okay, if life's treating him good.

And in 2024 we got back in contact, 20 years later. Wow.

We had a mutual friend who was in touch with both of us. I mentioned Butler one day, like, "Do you remember Benjamin Butler?" He said, "Yeah, got in contact with him a few months ago." And that was it—I had to reach out to bro.

Nothing had changed. We'd both thought of each other over the years. The conversation flowed like we had been speaking all that time. We told each other our stories, who we'd become. I'm proud of him—kids, book, trying to be a better person. Take my hat off to you, Butler.

And you know you got a brother for life.
Nuff love erry time.
Smid 😘 🤟🏿 "

Dribbz — Dribbz Talks Podcast

"Rapper, M.C and Men's mental health advocate Dribbz, first met Ben Butler when he invited Ben onto his 'Dribbz Talks' podcast platform to learn of his story, an encounter that neither of them expected would lead to anything more than a deep conversation. Yet, from that very first discussion, they discovered a shared passion for using their past and their experiences combined with music and  media to make a positive impact, particularly around issues like anti-knife crime and helping young people's mental health to express their emotions through lyrics. What started as a professional collaboration quickly blossomed into a genuine friendship as both sides instantly seen what could potentially be achieved in the future. With bags of passion and years of knowledge in their craft, it only made sense to link up. Since then, they have worked on numerous projects together, supporting youth empowerment and creative expression, Within a matter of months their bond has grown into something deeper—a brotherhood built on trust, shared purpose, and mutual respect.

Danielle John — Director, The EmpowHER Podcast

"I first came across Benny through social media, back when I was running my own podcast, #TellMeYourStory. I'd put out a post asking for people who wanted to share their lived experiences — not the sugar-coated version, but the raw truth of life: the mess, the mistakes, the moments you thought you'd never come back from. I was flooded with responses, but Benny's stood out. He didn't try to sound perfect or polished — he just sounded real. From the first conversation, I could tell he was someone who'd been through it, owned it, and turned it into something that could help others.

When we recorded Episode 5, "Benny Butler's Road to Redemption," I remember thinking this wasn't just another podcast episode — it was two people who had walked through fire and survived, sitting down and talking honestly about life, loss, and second chances. The energy was powerful. Benny talked about growing up without the right role models, surrounded by chaos, and how that eventually led to a series of choices that landed him in prison. But what struck me most was the way he spoke about change — not as some overnight miracle, but as a daily decision to do better, to be better, and to use his story to steer others away from the same mistakes.

That conversation has stayed with me ever since. It wasn't rehearsed or edited; it was real. Two people who'd both been through dark times, sharing space and reminding others that redemption is possible. You could feel the connection even through the screen — the honesty, the mutual respect, the shared understanding that sometimes the people who've made the biggest mistakes end up being the ones who make the biggest difference.

The episode ended up reaching nearly three thousand people, but what mattered wasn't the numbers — it was the messages that came after. People reached out to say they saw themselves in Benny's story. That they felt hope for the first time in a long time. That's what #TellMeYourStory was all about: creating a space where pain had purpose, where people's voices — the ones society often ignores — could finally be heard.

Since that time, my life's evolved in ways I could never have imagined. I've gone from recording stories to helping people write their own. I now lead the Cyfle Cymru project in Cardiff and the Vale, supporting people with substance use and mental health issues to move towards work and stability. And I've founded The

EmpowHER Project CIC — a women's empowerment organisation that helps women rebuild their lives after trauma, addiction, and prison. Every part of what I do today is built on the foundation of lived experience. I've sat in the cells, I've been at rock bottom, and I know how it feels to believe you're beyond saving — and I also know how powerful it is when someone says, "You're not."

That's why meeting Benny mattered. He represents what this whole movement is about — people who've lived it, learned from it, and now use it to light the way for others. Lived experience isn't just valuable; it's essential. It brings authenticity, empathy, and hope in ways textbooks never can. It bridges the gap between professionals and the people they're trying to reach. It proves that change isn't just possible — it's happening, every day, in people like Benny.

Looking back now, I realise that recording that episode wasn't just about sharing Benny's story — it was about connection. About two people who'd been broken but rebuilt themselves. About community, redemption, and the power of turning your past into your purpose. Benny's story continues to inspire, and I'll always be proud to have played a small part in helping the world hear it."

My Cousin Ben

"You walked into the room. I hadn't seen you since you were a baby, but I knew it was you… since that day, learning about your struggles I have just become more and more proud and in awe of you. Ben you are beautiful, unique and absolutely amazing! Don't let anyone lead you to believe any different. You are family, you are part of my family. Knowing you are in my life for life makes me very happy. I'm so proud of you, your determination, your strength and your resilience… I'm so proud of who you are despite everything you're kind-hearted, genuine and you always keep it real.

Love you loads and very proud x x

Ben Pugh — For Ben Butler

Healing From Being Hurt
Where do I begin.
My mental health.
The colour of my skin.
Or my position of wealth.

Where do I begin.
Where I have been.
Lines can become thin.
In judgement and what I've seen.

Where do I begin.
Strength in holding my head low.
And keeping up my chin.
Choosing where I go.

Where do I begin.
Learning from my past.
And teaching what's within.
Teaching lessons that last.

I begin with patience
An advising from what has hurt.
Helping a new generation.
Healing from being hurt.

Nina

"I still remember the day we first crossed paths at the David Lloyd gym during that personal training course. It was one of those moments that felt almost serendipitous, like the universe had conspired to bring two kindred spirits together. From the very first interaction, I sensed an easy camaraderie with Ben that was hard to come by.

He had this remarkable ability to listen intently, making me feel valued and understood. Whether discussing fitness techniques or life aspirations, Ben's support was unwavering. His encouragement often pushed me to dig deeper, to strive for my personal best, both in the gym and beyond.

In a world where connections can sometimes feel fleeting, meeting Ben felt like finding a true ally. Our shared passion for fitness quickly blossomed into a genuine friendship, one rooted in mutual respect and a desire for growth. As we navigated the ups and downs of our training journey together, I realized how fortunate I was to have someone like him by my side, always ready with a word of encouragement or a shared laugh.

Best Mate Joe Plomer

"Recently I attended a awards night with Ben, he was nominated for a community award and won.

It wasn't until later that evening I sat back and thought about how far he has come, 20 or even 10 years ago if you had told me that would be how we would spend our Friday evening I would of laughed.

Bens been my best friend since we met as young dumb teenagers and Watching grow into the man he is today fills my heart with so much pride it's difficult to put into words.

We have been by each others side and supported each other though The good the bad and the ugly but the thing that has stood firm is the love and care we have for each other.

As I always have and always will I'll stand with you and have your back whatever path life takes you on and thankfully now for us both it's a positive one.

I love you brother, always proud, always care, always here. keep moving forward 💙

GALLERY.

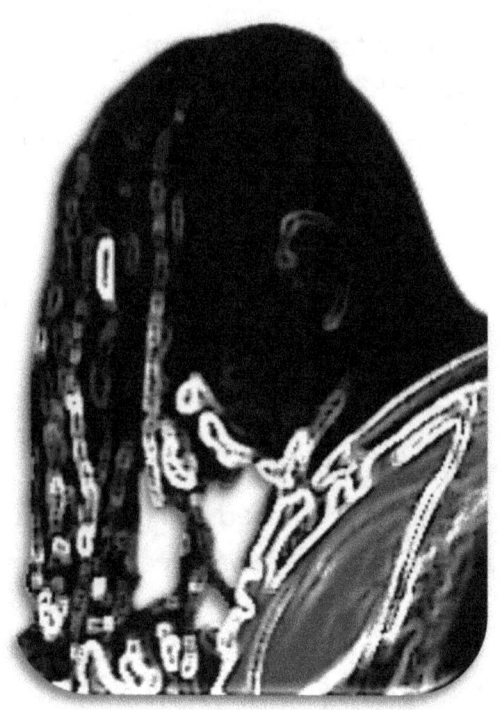

MISUNDERSTOOD

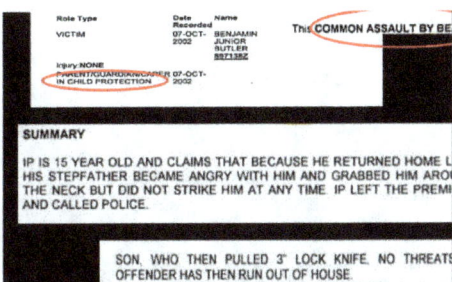

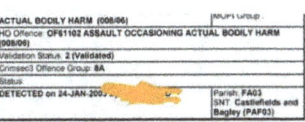

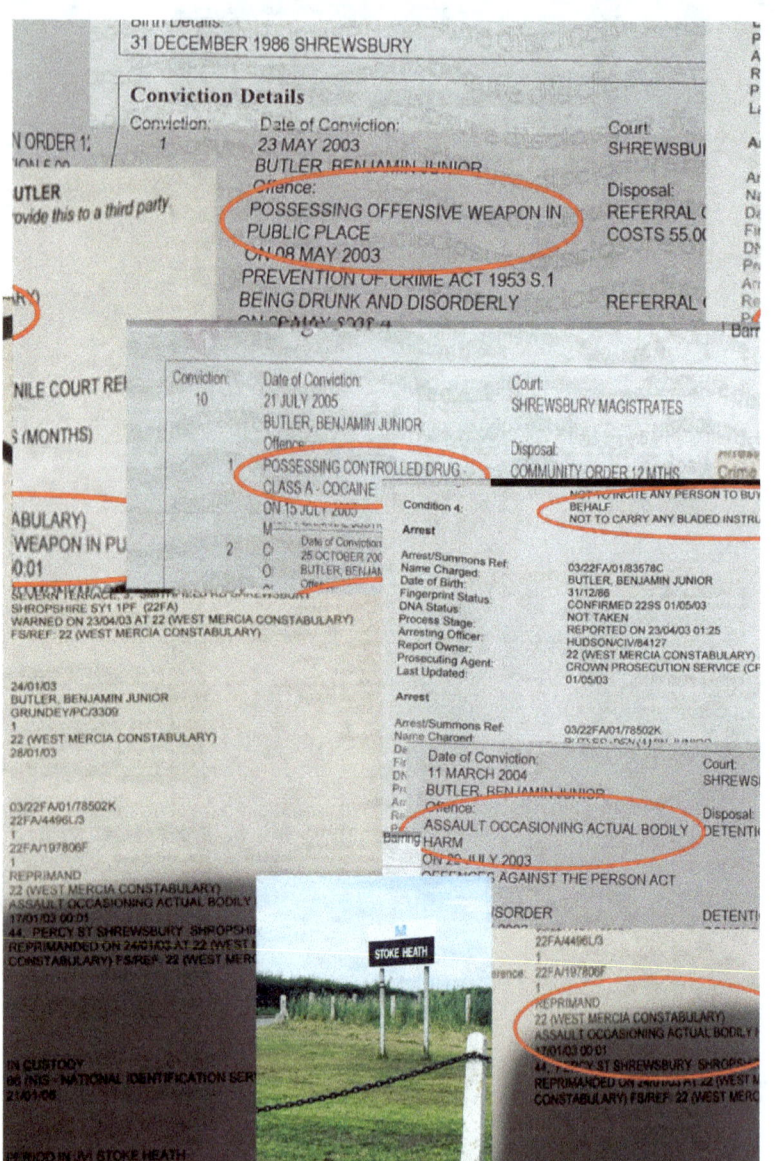

MISUNDERSTOOD

BEN J. BUTLER

TESTIMONIAL OF SERVICE

| Number | 30192666 | Rank | Gnr | Name | Butler | Regt/Corps | RA |

AFB 108 TESTIMONIAL 30192666 Gunner Butler

Gunner Butler joined the Army on 21 Apr 2014. Having completed his professional training at the Royal School of Artillery in Jan 2014 he was posted to 1st Regiment Royal Horse Artillery, a UK-based armoured artillery regiment equipped with 155 mm self-propelled guns.

Upon joining 1st Regiment Royal Horse Artillery, Gunner Butler started his career working as a signaller in the battery command post. This position requires the operator to develop an agile and adaptable mindset in what is a fast-paced working environment. An ability to deliver accurately and clearly under pressure are key requirements in the trade Gunner Butler has been working in. Gunner Butler has also proven himself to have be technically proficient in operating the requisite communications systems. He has demonstrated an understanding of the importance of equipment care and with clear direction is capable of working independently. Outside of his professional role Gunner Butler has played football for the Regiment.

Had he stayed in the Army, Gunner Butler would have been eligible to attend the Pre-Non-Commissioned Officers' Command, Leadership & Management Course. On completion of the course Gunner Butler could have been considered for promotion. This would have seen him step-up to lead and administer a small team of junior soldiers.

Gunner Butler is a mature character. He has carried out the work and duties expected of a

MISUNDERSTOOD

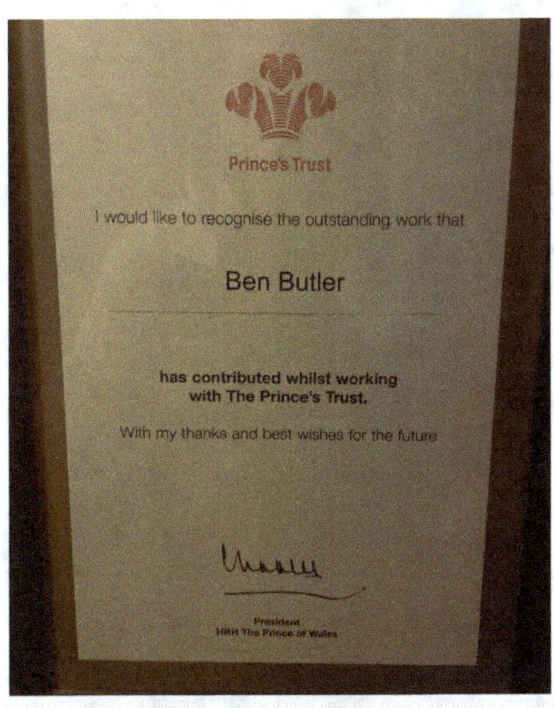

MISUNDERSTOOD

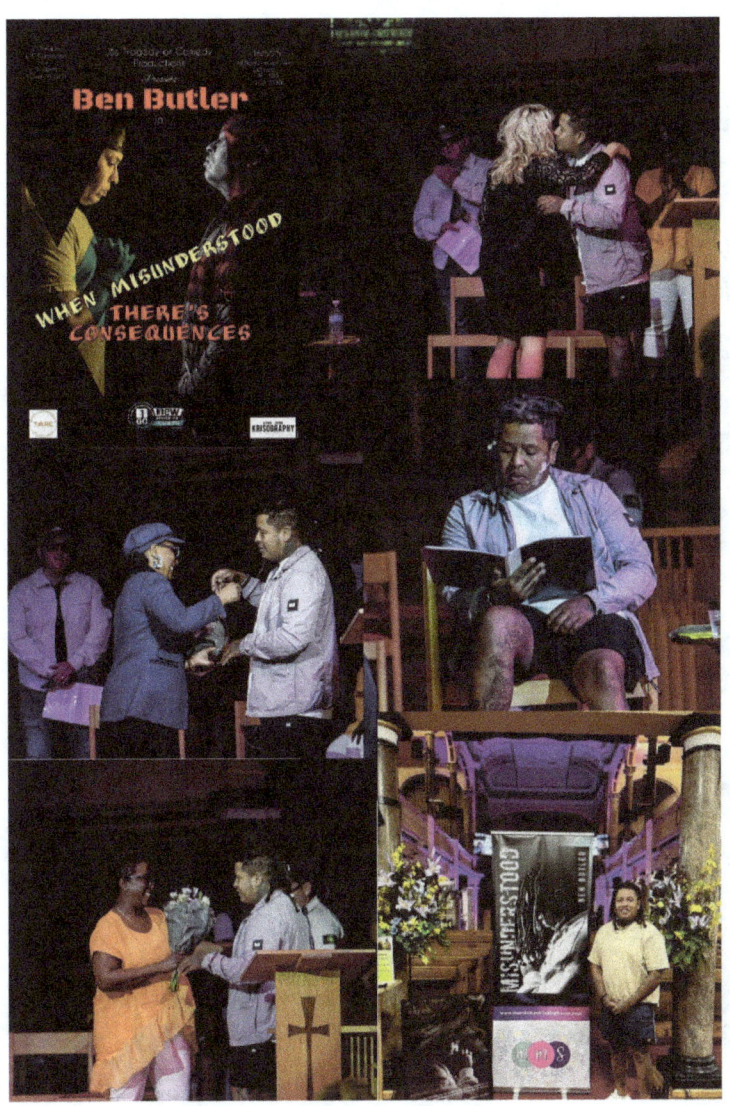

MISUNDERSTOOD

BEN J. BUTLER

Certificate of Completion

This certificate is awarded to

Ben Butler

who has successfully completed the online training course and assessment in:

Level 1 Child Criminal Exploitation and County Lines

Certificate Number: QFR5-Z5IQ-IRNQ-TFT3
Date: 08-Aug-2024

Signed: *Sarah Baker*
Sarah Baker, MD (Virtual College by Netex)

Virtual College Ltd, Marsel House, Stephensons Way, Ilkley LS29 8DD | virtual-college.co.uk

▶C Virtual College | by Netex

Certificate of Completion

This certificate is awarded to

Ben Butler

who has successfully completed the online training course and assessment in:

Level 1 Child Criminal Exploitation and County Lines

Certificate Number: QFR5-Z5IQ-IRNQ-TFT3
Date: 08-Aug-2024

Signed: *Sarah Baker*
Sarah Baker, MD (Virtual College by Netex)

Virtual College Ltd, Marsel House, Stephensons Way, Ilkley LS29 8DD | virtual-college.co.uk

MISUNDERSTOOD

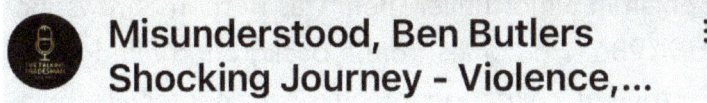

ABOUT THE AUTHOR

Benjamin Junior Butler (Ben) was born in Shrewsbury in 1986. He comes from a background filled with a turbulent childhood of physical and racial abuse. Having not had proper guidance and nurture at such a young age, Ben ended up in prison for choosing a wrong path in life. He was involved in Knife Crime, Violence, and Drugs. This resulted in a shattering blow to his mental health. Through ups and downs, he turned it all around. Since then, he has served in the Armed Forces and worked in a residential care home looking after vulnerable kids. Ben's organisation helps disengaged and at-risk youth. His goal is to inspire the New Generation and show that there is support and positive role models out there. Ben had and still has many bumps in the road with mental health issues, but he keeps on going. Because he wants his kids to see their dad is strong and has overcome many obstacles in life but refuses to back down. Ben wants to leave a positive legacy in his children, by making sure that they live and lead a better life than he had growing up. This is his journey so far! He is not looking for sympathy or forgiveness of others, as he has made peace with his past already and forgave himself for what he didn't know better. Ben's memoir, "Misunderstood," seeks to promote understanding of society's view of marginalised children.

www.marciampublishinghouse.com